The Charisma Guide

How To More Charismatic In All Areas
Of Your Life.
Learn The Skills of Charm To Be A
More Sociable and Likeable Person.

Tom Anderson & Angelina Williams

Copyright © Tom Anderson Publishing

Table of Contents

Introduction 6

What Is Charisma? 7

How Can I Become Charismatic?......................8

Chapter 1 – Defining Terms & The Big Restart 10

What Exactly Is Charisma? 10

What Makes Somebody Charismatic?...........................11

The Three Key Elements Of Charisma...........................12

Charisma Skills 15

There's More Than One Kind Of Charisma 16

Real Life Case Study – John...............................23

Chapter 2 –Your Charisma Levels...................................25

Easily Calculate Your Charisma Score...........................25

Quickly Develop Charisma Skills 28

Introvert or Extravert 29

Behaviors (Are You Sending Anti-Charisma Signals?).....31

Body Language To Avoid 32

Body Language To Captilize Upon 33

Do You Prepare Before Significant Events? 34

Charismatic Behaviors...............................35

What Do You Want To Achieve?...............................37

Chapter 3 – Exactly How to Fix Your Mindset................39

Mindset Changing Exercises 42

Real Life Case Study – Maria 47

Chapter 4 – Communication Skills...................................50

Assertive Communication...50

Other Communication Styles 52

Body Language 54

Active Listening..55

Real Life Case Study of Charismatic Communication 60

Chapter 5 – How To Talk To ANYONE..............................62

Communicating With Family & Friends...........................62

Generating Impactful Personal Conversations 64

Talking To Strangers...66

How To Actually Make Small Talk...................................66

Building Rapport 69

Talking To Colleagues, Clients, Or Superiors 70

Quickly Become Better at Written Communication........72

Chapter 6 – The Charisma Guide…It's Easier Than You
Think...77

Patience 77

Tolerance 79

Respect 81

Trust 81

Be Non-Judgmental 82

Humor 84

Honesty 85

How to Actually Develop Charismatic Personality Traits 87

How Do You Build Habits? 87

Chapter 7 – Charismatic Body Language 91

Observe The Body Language Of Charismatic People 92

Positive Body Language Signifiers 98

Facial Expressions & Eye Contact 100

Body Language Combined with Effective Speaking 102

Real Life Case Study – Janine 102

Chapter 8 – Communicating at Work 105

Being Both Professional & Personable 107

Charismatic Work Behaviors 113

Real Life Case Study – Hunter 116

Chapter 9 – Powerful Conversations with Anyone 118

Influencing 121

Motivating 122

Directing & Controlling Conversations 123

Closing Powerful Conversations 127

Chapter 10 – Managing Conflict Charismatically 130

Handling Conflict 133

Apologizing Charismatically *137*

Conclusion *142*

Introduction

When you hear the word charisma, you probably already have someone in mind who embodies that term for you. We all know someone with charisma, who commands the attention of a room the moment they walk in. These individuals can captivate, inspire, and influence others – seemingly without trying. Charismatic individuals are instantly likable, and people seem to fall over themselves to gain their notice or approval.

It's easy to believe that charisma is some in-built superpower that a lucky few are just born with, while the rest of us mere mortals are doomed only to admire them. Luckily, that's not true. Charisma is a skill – or set of skills – that can be learned and applied to help you become more successful at inspiring and influencing others.

But What Does Charisma Look Like?

Let's take the example of Tom Cruise, who is widely regarded as one of the most charismatic men in Hollywood. What is it that makes Tom stand out over and above other actors as more charismatic? He's certainly not managed to avoid controversy altogether – remember him jumping wildly on Oprah's couch? Yet that incident and any other criticism roll off him like water off a duck's back, and people remain captivated with him whenever he speaks.

Most of the actors and directors who've worked with Tom are incredibly complimentary about him and describe how working with him makes them feel incredible. His acting colleagues almost always have a story about how Tom put them at ease and made them feel like he took a genuine interest in them as a person.

This is the key thing about charisma – in many ways, is it's not about you. You're looking to engage and involve others rather than dazzle them with your brilliance. Even stood on a stage delivering a speech to hundreds of people, a speaker with charisma is the one who can make the audience feel as though this is an intimate chat, speaking to them as if on a personal level.

Throughout history, the most influential and successful people seem to have a similar way of presenting this kind of magnetic personality to others. It may appear to be a rare natural ability, but it's something anybody can achieve as long as they're willing to put the time in, be patient, and practice.

What Is Charisma?

The word charisma is used all the time, but ask somebody to define it in words, and most people won't have a succinct answer. There are lots of terms that are used to describe charisma and people that are charismatic. For example, mystique, joie de vivre, allure, and having the 'X' factor, are all used to imply charisma - among many others.

People might describe it as having a magnetic personality, being charming, or someone who commands attention - but these descriptions also don't fully capture what it means to be charismatic. We'll explore this in more detail in Chapter 1, but the best way I have heard charisma described is as a way of generating positive energy in other people.

One way to look at it is that charisma is a collection of sophisticated social and emotional skills. People with these skills have the ability to stir strong emotions in others while also projecting exceptional calm, confidence, and focus.

How Can I Become Charismatic?

If you've always wanted to be charismatic but believed that it was something you either had or you didn't, then you're in luck. It might seem like an ethereal personality trait, but charisma is simply a set of skills that can be learned if you are willing to put the time and effort to learn it.

As charisma is a set of skills, it's absolutely possible to learn how to become charismatic by gaining or strengthening particular skills. You'll begin by making conscious choices to adjust your behavior, which might feel a little forced initially, but they will start to feel natural over time. Even better, making these new behaviors a true habit means that after a while, you will do them without having to think about them at all.

You don't have to make a drastic change to who you are; you merely have to implement these skills in a way that feels comfortable for you. If you currently consider yourself uncharismatic, then practicing these skills at first may feel strange. Of course, any new behaviors feel a little unnatural as you begin to implement them, but they should feel like they can become part of you and your personality. Riding a bike would have felt a little unnatural when you first learned, but now it's as easy as, well, riding a bike!

There's no one way to be charismatic. There are a certain set of behaviors and skills that you can implement to be charismatic, but you don't need to employ them all, all of the time in every situation. One of the biggest keys to becoming charismatic is to find a way to do it that feels natural to you.

At first, you won't necessarily feel charismatic, but you should notice people beginning to respond to you more positively. You'll be making conscious choices to adjust your behavior. Even better, making these new behaviors a true habit means that they will become part of you after a while without thinking about them at all.

So, relax into adopting the techniques you learn throughout this book and don't be afraid to modify them just a little to complement your own unique personality. The aim is to bring out the charisma you are already capable of, not to become an entirely new person. If you're trying to suddenly morph into a different person with different interests and values, you won't come across as charismatic or authentic – you'll come across as phony, hollow, and maybe even a little egotistical. And people immediately see through that.

The purpose of this book is to guide you through the process of becoming more charismatic. We'll start with understanding what charisma is (and isn't), followed by actionable tips to become more charismatic.

To begin we'll define some of the terms that we'll use in the book, look closer at what charisma is, and how charismatic you are right now in your regular interactions with others.

Chapter 1 – Defining Terms & The Big Restart

"The reason we're successful, darling? My overall charisma, of course."
Freddie Mercury

What Exactly *Is* Charisma?

Charisma is always valuable, but it's practically essential to be successful in some careers. Politics, acting, and presenting are all areas where charisma gives you a serious edge, and lacking charisma can mean your career never gets off the ground.

This idea of charisma as something people have or don't have can make it seem like some people are born charismatic. In truth, we're all born with the capability to become charismatic. For some people, the skills they learn from their parents or their combination of personality traits naturally combine perfectly to produce a charismatic person. It's not magic; it's a set of learned behaviors.

For others, they practice those skills slowly and eventually learn to become charismatic.

As we've discussed, charisma is made up of a set of skills. If you have some of those skills, you'll have some level of charisma already. If you have all of them? You're effectively Tom Cruise. So, if developing charisma seems complicated, then just look at the skills you already have and hone them before moving on to form the ones you don't. Take it slowly, and make it fun. Developing charisma is an enjoyable journey that can take you to new heights of success you never believed were possible.

At its core, Charisma is simply a way to connect with people through the power of your own personality. You'll find many hairdressers and estheticians have charisma. They'll often have developed or at least honed that charisma through their job because it involves a lot of connection and communication with their clients.

The same can be said of salespeople. Not all salespeople have charisma, but the successful ones usually have it in spadefuls because connecting with people is how you sell. People buy from people, not from businesses. Charisma makes people want to do what you want them to do.

There's more than one way to be charismatic too. Often what we perceive as charisma is a combination of overwhelmingly positive communication behaviors. There are specific skills that make you more charismatic. You can apply those skills in different ways depending on the situation or your own natural preferences.

What Makes Somebody Charismatic?

It's undeniable that confidence plays a part in being charismatic. It's difficult to hold people's attention or get them to believe in you if you don't come across as self-confident.

We often think of charismatic people as attractive, well-groomed, and physically fit. And these things can help you project confidence but are not essential to being charismatic. You definitely don't have to look a particular way to have charisma. However, a basic standard of grooming and personal hygiene is necessary. In fact, merely being charismatic can make people rate you as more attractive.

The Three Key Elements Of Charisma

Charisma is both incredibly complex and incredibly simple at the same time, and it's something psychologists and behavioral scientists have been studying for years. One of the common ways it's broken down into an understandable format is splitting it into three key elements.

Presence
Presence doesn't just mean being able to command the attention of a room. It also means being fully present in a situation. Charismatic people are entirely present in the moment. Being wholly present brings their full attention and focus on the conversation they are having, which does two important things. It allows them to focus on what is being said and what is happening and respond accordingly. This type of presence is crucial because it makes the person they are speaking to feel important and valued.

Have you ever heard the old saying that people don't remember what you said, but they remember how you made them feel? Being present at every conversation and meeting you attend will make people feel valued. It will make them like and remember you more.

This is one of the fundamental skills that charismatic people have. They give others their full focus instead of allowing themselves to be distracted. They make you feel important because they actively listen to you, and they are interested in what you have to say. It's quite a rare thing for someone to be completely focused on you – and when it happens, you almost instantly connect with that person.

We'll cover focus and presence in more detail later in the book under communication and mindset. But for now, don't worry if you recognize that you find it hard to focus entirely on what people say. It's a common trait, and surprisingly a hangover from our caveman days. The primitive part of our brain is on constant alert for threats, and it's easily distracted. If you haven't yet learned techniques to shut it off, then you're not alone. In some situations, being easily distracted is vital to survival. However, in others, it can make you a lot less likable and hinders your ability to form connections.

Now that you know that it's essential, you can start to train your brain to remain concentrated. This can be done by practicing meditation and mindfulness – which we'll explore in more detail in Chapter 3. In time, and with practice, you'll find it much easier to focus on one thing for some time. Not only will it make you more charismatic – it can make you more productive too!

Power
You don't need to be a CEO, Hollywood superstar, the President of the United States, or incredibly rich to have enough power to be charismatic. The perception of power

can come from something as small as your ability to influence others or your knowledge of a particular subject matter. Physical strength and social status are also indicators of power that can add to your charisma.

When people perceive you as powerful, they will automatically grant you a specific authority and respect that is an integral part of the charisma puzzle.

Warmth

Warmth is what makes you likable, and it comes from a genuine connection with others, empathy, and compassion.

Warmth is a combination of many different traits. People who are perceived as warm are usually authentic, demonstrate a genuine interest in others, and don't tend to gossip. They're trustworthy, and you feel like they have your best interests at heart. When someone displays warmth, they make you feel good about yourself, and you feel like opening up and speaking to them.

Most importantly, to note, all of these charisma elements are chiefly assessed through non-verbal means. It's often not what you say; it's how you say it and what is conveyed through your body language that matters the most. So, suppose you're the type of person who struggles with making conversation. In that case, it might be reassuring to realize that you can become more charismatic without even saying a single word.

That's not to say that your words don't matter. You can enhance or harm your charisma with the words you say. Still, on the whole, you can recover more quickly from saying the wrong thing with the right body language and intonation than you can from saying the right thing but getting the non-verbal elements wrong.

Similarly significant is that it's the combination of these elements that makes someone charismatic. An abundance of warmth without power or presence will make you likable but not incredibly charismatic. Likewise, being remarkably present and projecting power without warmth will make you intimidating rather than charismatic.

Charisma Skills

Another way to break down charisma into specific parts is to separate them out into particular skill areas. That way, you can identify which skills you already have and where you need to improve. Each skill links directly to one of the three elements of charisma above.

Emotional Expressiveness – Charismatic people are good at expressing their feelings spontaneously, usually in a positive way. The emotions they display will appear genuine to others, which makes them attractive. They are adept at showing positive emotions like gratitude and joy in an almost infectious manner.

Emotional Sensitivity – Charismatic people are good at reading the emotions of others and responding accordingly – which encourages emotional connection. They always seem to know just what to say. This is because they are excellent at picking up on the little emotional and behavioral cues others unconsciously give.

Emotional Control – Charismatic people can control and regulate their emotions. They only display the feelings they want you to see, and they show them in the most effective way possible.

Social Expressiveness – Charismatic people interact socially with ease. They are excellent conversationalists who choose their words and body language carefully.

Social Sensitivity – Charismatic people are adept at reading and interpreting social situations, listening attentively to others, and getting on others' wavelengths.

Social Control – Charismatic people are excellent at fitting in in any social setting. They know how to adapt their behaviors to be accepted by almost any group of people.

There's More Than One Kind Of Charisma

We use 'charisma' as a catch-all term for people who can seemingly effortlessly engage with and inspire others. But there's no one way to be charismatic. We discussed the three charisma elements a moment ago, and you indeed need all three aspects in combination to be considered charismatic. However, the way you blend those elements can result in very different kinds of charisma.

When you project high power with lower presence and warmth, you're displaying authority charisma. High warmth and presence with lower power is personality charisma. You will find that one may be more suited to particular situations over another. Also, some will come more naturally than others to you, depending on your own personality type.

Personality Types

Your personality is a combination of your behavior, characteristics, attitude, and style. These unique attributes combine to make you the person you are. Personality isn't static, although it's often shaped quite early in our lives. Various factors influence your nature - including your family background, life experiences, social status, current environment, and education.

We've discussed how different personality types might be more naturally suited to displaying certain types of charisma. But how do you figure out your personality type to make sure you get the best out of your charisma?

There are various personality profiling methodologies, but one of the most widely known and used is Myers Briggs, so let's look at that one to help you find out.

Myers-Briggs Personality Types

One of the most popular personality profiling tools is Myers-Briggs. If you don't know your Myers Briggs type, there are numerous resources online where you can complete a quiz, and it will bring back your personality type.

The types are a combination of letters that tell you if you are:

- **Introverted (I) or Extroverted (E)** – This is where you focus your attention and gain energy.
- **Intuitive (N) or Sensing (S)** – This is how you absorb information.
- **Thinking (T) or Feeling (F)** – This is how you process information.
- **Judging (J) or Perceiving (P)** – This is how you deal with the world.

So, an INFJ is introverted, intuitive, feeling, and judging.

Myers-Briggs is useful to get an idea of how you come across to other people now, and they can be reasonably accurate. However, if your personality type doesn't seem very charismatic, don't worry. People can change from one type to another, depending on their circumstances and situation.

Here's a brief breakdown of the various Myers-Briggs types and how charismatic they tend to be.

Personality Types With More Natural Charismatic Ability:
Unsurprisingly, almost all of the Extroverted personality types tend to be more charismatic. Still, a pleasant surprise is that several Introverted types also make the most charismatic list.

Introverted Intuitive Feeling Judging – INFJs are introverts who don't tend to seek out the company of others. Yet, they can be surprisingly charismatic when they do interact with others. They are particularly good at communicating due to their way with words that captivates the attention of others. INFJ can often fall down by presenting themselves as powerful or demonstrating a high level of warmth.

Extroverted Intuitive Feeling Judging – ENFJs are often good entertainers, and their ability to pick up on others' emotional cues makes them good at projecting warmth in particular. They have a way about them that makes other people feel good. They tend to command people's attention, which gives them a certain charismatic air that's difficult to resist.

Extroverted Intuitive Feeling Perceiving – ENFPs are very good at using their charm to persuade others. Still, they can occasionally be prone to bouts of social awkwardness. On the whole, they are very engaging and excellent at making others feel listened to, and they can come across as very charismatic – especially if talking about an idea they feel passionate about.

Introverted Intuitive Thinking Judging – INTJs tend to be introverted but very intelligent, making them seem charismatic when they are interested in the topic they are speaking about.

Introverted Intuitive Feeling Perceiving – INFPs have a great sense of humor, which in the right circumstances can make them charismatic. They are also excellent listeners and adept at making people feel understood – another vital characteristic of charismatic people.

Extroverted Intuitive Thinking Judging – ENTJs are often excellent at authority charisma. They often seem larger than life and are very outgoing. They aren't always good at listening to others and can sometimes make people feel like it's their way or the highway.

Extroverted Intuitive Thinking Perceiving – ENTPs are brilliant at reading people. Combined with their sense of humor and honed communication skills, they tend to have an effortlessly charismatic way about them.

Extroverted Sensing Feeling Judging – ESFJs are very empathetic, which makes them rate highly for warmth. They are usually very popular and outgoing and can come across as very charismatic.

Extroverted Sensing Thinking Perceiving – ESTPs are usually very charismatic. Their way with words and the ability to make others feel special makes them magnetic. They are very energetic and love socializing.

Personality Types With Lesser Built In Charisma: People with these personality types are less likely to come across as naturally charismatic. However, with the right skills and some practice, they can become as charismatic as any other personality type. If you are one of the following personality types, you can absolutely learn how to develop charisma.

Introverted Intuitive Thinking Perceiving – INTPs tend to live very internal lives and rarely come across as charismatic. They are very easily distracted and can sometimes seem like they aren't really listening to people.

Introverted Sensing Thinking Judging – ISTJs are very focused, but they also have a certain amount of warmth that makes them likable. They are huge believers in duty and responsibility, and their focused nature makes them good listeners too.

Extroverted Sensing Thinking Judging – ESTJs are outgoing and confident but can come across as lacking warmth or having a genuine interest in others. They sometimes come across as being self-involved, but they are usually quite entertaining and the life of the party.

Introverted Sensing Feeling Judging – ISFJs are warm and generous, which makes them likable, but they can lack self-confidence and tend to be quite introverted.

Introverted Sensing Thinking Perceiving – ISTPs tend to

avoid interacting with others and are not often likely to be interested in appearing charismatic. They are factual and can be seen as rather blunt. But their devil-may-care attitude when it comes to how others view them makes them seem edgy and cool and lends a charismatic air to them.

Introverted Sensing Feeling Perceiving – ISFPs tend to be quiet and shy but are very attuned to others' feelings and are quite empathetic. They are likable but don't have much self-confidence and don't enjoy a lot of social interaction.

Extroverted Sensing Feeling Perceiving – ESFPs are generally the center of attention wherever they go and are rarely shy or socially awkward. That confidence makes people warm to them. As ESFPs rarely take themselves too seriously, their sense of humor is also a draw.

Knowing your Myers Briggs personality type allows you to understand how other people may perceive you. However, to get the most out of learning your personality type, you need to be totally honest when answering the questions. There are no right or wrong answers, so base your answers on how you most often behave or react and try to be as objective as possible.

Myers Briggs is probably the most popular personality profiling tool, but it's not the only one. Another popular tool is the Enneagram.

Enneagram
The Enneagram identifies nine different personality types:

The Reformer – is a perfectionist type who has a lot of emotional control but may lack the warmth to be truly charismatic.

The Helper – is incredibly warm and caring, with a strong urge to please people. They have a lot of warmth but may lack the emotional control to be truly charismatic.

The Achiever – is incredibly driven, self-confident, and focused on success. They are very conscious of their image and are the most naturally charismatic enneagram type.

The Individualist – is very introverted but can have a tendency to be dramatic. They are very emotionally expressive but tend to lack emotional control and awareness.

The Investigator – is highly intelligent and can be very emotionally aware. Still, they are also quite introverted and can lack warmth.

The Loyalist – is very responsible and can be quite charming. They have a tendency to anxiety that can prevent them from being charismatic. Still, if they have high emotional control, they are very capable of being charismatic.

The Enthusiast – is always on the go, highly spontaneous, and fun to be around. They're the party's life and soul, but they are easily distracted and can struggle to be fully present in the moment.

The Challenger – is very confident and assertive but can tend to be confrontational and aggressive, which can stand in the way of them being considered charismatic.

The Peacemaker – is easygoing and very agreeable. Although they are easy to get along with, they are often self-deprecating. They can come across as lacking in confidence.

You can discover your Enneagram type by taking a short online quiz, and there are many free versions available.

One great thing about understanding personality types is that it helps you become better at responding to people in a way that suits them best and can make you a better communicator with others – an essential charisma skill. If you can identify their personality type, you'll be able to adjust your communication style to suit other's preferences better. Just using this simple skill can dramatically increase the chances that they will find you charismatic.

Real Life Case Study – John

John was not what you would consider charismatic in high school and college. He got average grades, had a reasonably large circle of friends, and was generally well-liked. Still, he didn't have the ability to hold the attention of a room, and he lacked public speaking skills. If he had to speak in public, he would get incredibly nervous and forget lines or spend most of the time looking at the floor.

After John graduated, he took a job as a field sales rep for a major software company. He was good at his job but quickly realized that he needed to develop his charisma to be the best salesperson he could be. He was hitting his targets but rarely exceeding them, which could hold him back in his career.

As part of a team-building exercise, he completed the Myers-Briggs personality profiling test. He learned that he was an Introverted Intuitive Feeling Perceiving (INFP). He had some of the building blocks of charisma, such as being a generally good listener and being fully present in the moment. However, he needed to work on being more empathetic, self-confident and projecting more power.

He studied charisma and identified which skills he needed to work on. He worked on developing more emotional awareness and emotional sensitivity so that he could improve his warmth. He also made subtle changes to his workwear and posture to project a more powerful image.

John started to close clients that he wouldn't normally have closed before, landed bigger deals, and exceeded his sales targets by developing the aforementioned skills and behaviors. He also noticed that he became a more popular team member as his colleagues were naturally drawn to his new, more charismatic nature.

Like John, some of the skills and behaviors you already have may well be charismatic. In fact, you may be surprised to learn that you're not starting from ground zero when it comes to developing charisma. And no matter what your starting point, you can always develop charisma. In Chapter 2, we'll take a look at how to assess your current charisma levels.

Chapter 2 –Your Charisma Levels

"We shouldn't require our politicians to be movie stars. Then again, we're all influenced by charisma. It's hard not to be. We all collectively fall for it."
Julianne Moore

We've already seen that your Myers-Briggs personality type can give you an idea of how others perceive you, including how charismatically you come across. However, one of the problems with completing a self-assessment is that you are answering based on what you think, and sometimes others do not see us in the way we see ourselves. Plus, charisma is such a difficult thing to define. We know it when we see it, but breaking it down into its building blocks can be very difficult.

In this chapter, we'll take a look at assessing your current charisma levels beyond Myers-Briggs or other personality type models. You will do this by breaking down the charisma elements and evaluating where you are on that scale. To some extent, this is still subjective but should provide a more in-depth analysis of your current charisma levels.

Easily Calculate Your Charisma Score

We discussed earlier the six essential skills associated with charisma. Answer these simple yes/no questions to identify which skills you have and where you might land on the charisma scale. For each 'yes,' give yourself one point:

Social Sensitivity
- Are you comfortable with social etiquette?
- Do you consider your words before you speak?
- Do people say you are a good listener?
- Do you always ensure to present yourself well in social environments?
- Do you pay attention to other people in your environment?

Social Control
- Do other people consider you to be self-confident?
- Do you find it easy to get along with all kinds of people?
- Do you naturally take the lead in a group?
- Do you find making conversation with strangers easy?
- Is it rare for you to feel awkward or flustered in a social situation?

Social Expressiveness
- Do you feel comfortable, even when around people you don't know?
- Are you able to easily participate in conversations on many different topics?
- Do you take the initiative of introducing yourself to new people?
- Do you consider yourself to be an excellent public speaker?
- Do others consider you outgoing and extroverted?

Emotional Sensitivity

- Do you often empathize closely with what other people feel?
- Can you easily read other people's emotions, even if they are trying to hide them?
- Do your friends feel that you genuinely listen and care about their problems?
- Are you considered a calming person?
- Do others often mention how you just seem to 'get' them?

Emotional Control
- Can you easily hide your real emotion from others if you want to?
- Do people look to you for reassurance in stressful situations?
- Are you able to express your emotions on cue?
- Are you able to remain calm and collected even when others are panicking?
- Do you believe that people often can't tell what you're feeling inside?

Emotional Expressiveness
- Are you considered the life and soul of the party?
- Have others told you that you have an expressive face?
- Is it difficult for you to keep your face blank and expressionless?
- Do people consider you to be a very energetic person?
- Are you tactile with people when you're talking?

If you scored over 20, you would likely be considered charismatic. 25-30 is highly charismatic.

It's common to be stronger in one or two of the above charisma elements than the others, but ideally, you want a balance across them. Lacking skills in any section can harm your charisma. For example, someone with high emotional control but low emotional sensitivity can come across as disingenuous rather than charismatic because they don't project the warmth needed to balance it. High emotional expressiveness without high emotional control can make you seem erratic or 'hyper.'

Quickly Develop Charisma Skills

If you're scoring low on the above charisma quiz or want to brush up on the sections you lack in, here are some quick tips to boost your charisma:

Confidence/Anxiety
Self-confidence is essential to being charismatic. If you're constantly questioning yourself, this will show in your body language and facial expressions. Anxiety and being unsure of yourself makes it difficult for people to warm to you because they will – often unconsciously – pick up on your unease. When that happens, people will often assume that they are making you feel uneasy rather than a general lack of confidence on your part. And this can make them feel bad and thus uneasy around you. People draw to them those who make them feel good about themselves, so it's challenging to be charismatic if your anxiety unintendedly makes people feel distressed.

Of course, even charismatic people have to deal with some anxiety and knocks to their self-confidence at times – that's simply part and parcel of being human. However, being able to tame and control this anxiety is essential to coming across as consistently charismatic.

Awareness of Others/Interpersonal Intelligence
Being charismatic involves making others feel good about themselves. Doing that means picking up on small signals that give you clues and insight into their emotions and thoughts. It also means correctly listening so that you are present and able to respond appropriately.

As we discussed briefly earlier, appropriate responses are about more than saying the right words. Your body language can make the most significant difference in how people respond to you.

Influence & Persuasion
The power aspect of charisma means being able to influence and persuade others. There are many ways to achieve this, and if you don't have any apparent authority or power, sometimes warmth is the key to opening up power. Being likable means people are more likely to want to do things for you, which makes you able to influence them and, in turn, makes you powerful.

Introvert or Extravert

Are you an introvert or an extrovert? We touched upon this briefly as part of our exploration of personality types in Chapter 1. The concept of introverts and extroverts as we know it began with psychologist Carl Jung in 1920.

Extroverts may seem to have an easier time developing charisma, but that doesn't mean that introverts aren't or can't become charismatic. Introverts often have a hidden advantage: they are the best listeners and tend to think before speaking.

But What Does Being An Introvert Or An Extrovert Mean?

In a nutshell, extroverts are energized by social interaction and depleted by time spent alone. Introverts re-energize through time spent alone and can find social interactions intense and draining. That's not to say that extroverts never need some alone time, or introverts hate every social activity, but too much of those activities can leave them feeling drained.

Most of us are comfortable describing ourselves as introverts or extroverts. Still, most of us are really ambiverts – capable of 'flexing' along the extroversion introversion scale and depending on a range of factors. Getting too hung up on the idea of yourself as at one end of the scale can hamper your self-development.

It's a common misconception that only extroverts are charismatic, but that's not true at all. There are different ways of being charismatic, and being an introvert is not a barrier to developing charisma. Extroverts can have a definite advantage, but introverts can also be incredibly charismatic. And despite our insistence that we are one or the other – most of us are ambiverts and capable of moving between the two types as the situation necessitates.

Behaviors (Are You Sending Anti-Charisma Signals?)

The right behaviors and body language can drastically boost your charisma signals. But the wrong actions and body language act as anti-charisma signals.

How Do You React In Certain Situations?
Charismatic people are generally thoughtful and poised. They avoid harmful or over-reactions, and the most charismatic people are adept at avoiding any accidental negativity.

People latch on to negativity; unfortunately, it's human hardwiring to take the most notice of something that could be threatening or bad. So when you say things like 'no problem,' people hone in on the 'problem' part, despite the positive intentions. Charismatic people say something in a positive and specific manner that leaves no room for ambiguity.

We'll cover this in much more detail in Chapter 3, but paying attention to how positively you speak and react can help you become more aware of the messages you are sending others about your mindset and who you are.

What Signals Do You Send Via Body Language?
It may surprise you to learn that most of your communication isn't via the words you use. Others will place more value in using your body language to interpret your message's meaning than they will your words. So being mindful and aware of your body language can help

you become instantly more charismatic.

Another good reason to develop an understanding of body language is to read and react to other people's emotions more effectively and thus increase your warmth perception to others. Understanding body language gives you a significant insight into what others may be thinking or feeling.

Body Language To Avoid

If you want to come across as more charismatic, avoid these body-language signals that make you appear anxious:

Fidgeting – For example, clicking a pen, tapping a foot, tapping your fingers on a table.

Yawning – It can make it seem like you aren't listening or interested in what people are saying.

Constant Scanning – Looking around the room and avoiding eye contact.

Fussing with your clothing – For example, adjusting a tie, smoothing down a skirt, picking lint from clothing

Folded or crossed arms

Hunched shoulders

Tense muscles – a big giveaway of feeling nervous.

Body Language To Captilize Upon

These body language signals help send out the message that you are relaxed and confident. They are the body language signals that you would expect to see from charismatic individuals. By consciously adopting some of these when speaking, you will automatically come across as more confident and charismatic.

Smiling – A warm, genuine smile that shows the teeth makes you look confident and relaxed. It also helps put others at ease. Genuine smiles reach your eyes, making them crinkle slightly at the corners.

Good eye contact – Steady eye contact is one of the best ways to appear assertive and confident. If you are reluctant to make eye contact at all, you will come across as nervous or maybe even untrustworthy.

Leaning slightly forward – When speaking, it makes the people you talk to feel as though you're sharing something important. On the other hand, when someone else is talking, it can make them feel all the focus is on them, and you're paying close attention.

Keep your shoulders back and relaxed, and your chin parallel to the floor – This action indicates that someone is comfortable in their skin and feels that they belong. Making this your default posture is a quick way to appear instantly more confident and charismatic.

These are not exhaustive lists, but they're good starter points to improve your body language. Another great habit of getting into is to watch charismatic people's body language and to try mirroring it.

Do You Prepare Before Significant Events?

Preparing for situations where you want to be incredibly charismatic – like a job interview, first date, or school reunion – is essential. You'll want to take the time to get into the right mindset for the occasion and work through exercises to reduce the uncomfortable feelings you have about the situation. If you don't do this, your conscious or subconscious feelings will leak into your body language.

People often overlook the time needed to decompress or get into the right mindset between one situation and another. For example, say you have a job interview to leave a highly stressful or unfulfilling job to start a new exciting career. Well, suppose you go straight from your stressful job into an interview situation. In that case, you're going to be carrying some lingering stress from the workplace situation you just left. Your body language and thinking you display during your interview will reflect your stress. Unfortunately, this will not help you appear charismatic when you need it most.

Taking time to decompress by doing something relaxing and putting yourself in the right frame of mind for an interview will alleviate this. What works best for you will be personal. For example, some might play a motivating playlist of uplifting music to shift into the right mindset. Music can positively boost your mood and attitude.

Listening to music that you associate with success or fun experiences can help you recapture those feelings, almost as though you were back in the moment.

For others, an hour in a quiet place, writing in a journal, or using mindfulness meditation is the best choice for them. Gratitude journals can be particularly useful for helping you to get into the right mindset for a situation. And the benefits of meditation are well-studied and highly impressive. We'll cover some simple meditations you can do in Chapter 3.

Visualizing a successful outcome can also make a real difference to how you feel and the signals you send out in a particular situation. If you find yourself thinking of ways that it might go wrong, stop and start to imagine exactly how it would go if it all went perfectly. Walking into any situation in the right frame of mind and feeling prepared can make a huge difference in how well you can project confidence and appear charismatic.

Charismatic Behaviors

Here are some of the most charismatic personality traits:

Actively listening – Active listening is when you focus entirely on the person you are communicating with and don't allow any internal or external distractions. By simply listening, you make the person feel unique and valued. There is no need to add your viewpoint or give them your judgment unless they ask for it.

Treating everyone with respect – Charismatic people aren't forceful or pushy. They have an uncanny ability to persuade and influence people, but they do this by making people want to do what they ask of them. Achieving others' respect is almost always accomplished by making people feel listened to and valued – and nothing makes people feel more relevant than when treated with complete respect.

Frequently smiling – We discussed above how smiling is a powerful body language signal for being charismatic. Smiling helps your charisma in two ways. It not only puts other people at ease and makes you appear warmer. It also makes you feel happier and more confident. Simply smiling sends a signal to your brain that makes you feel happier, even when you may not be overly optimistic.

Making a point of remembering people's names and small details – Using the 'fine print' of people is another marked way of making people feel special. Remember that being charismatic has more to do with the way you make people feel than anything else. When you make a point of remembering people's names and remembering little details about them – like where they went on vacation or their children's names, it makes them feel like you are paying attention to them.

Accepting and delivering compliments in a genuine way – When people give you compliments, do you accept them graciously, or do you brush them off? When you don't accept a compliment, it can make the person complimenting you feel bad about themselves, but positively taking it makes them feel good. Giving thoughtful and genuine compliments is also a great way to make people feel special.

Again, these are not the full gambit of ways to become more charismatic. However, if you can tick most of these off simple acts as behaviors that you display, or make a conscious effort to show them, then you're well on the way to being charismatic.

What Do You Want To Achieve?

If you've picked up a book on charisma, then it's an area that interests you. But why do you want to improve your appeal? Your motivation for developing your charisma can help you understand which type of charm you need to build to get the best results.

Do you want to create better first impressions socially and in job interviews?

Are you looking to develop career success using charisma to help you negotiate and influence your way to the top of the ladder? Perhaps you want to create better first impressions? Or achieve more social success? To tap into your charisma potential, you'll need to understand what's driving you. What are your motivations and your fears?

As we've seen, there are different kinds of charisma, including authority charisma and personal charisma. While the skills are broadly the same for these two types of charisma, understanding what you want to achieve will help you know what to focus on first. For personal charisma, warmth should be a key focus. For authority charisma, presence and power are essential.

Now you should know what charisma is, what you want to achieve by becoming more charismatic, and how charismatic you currently are. Next, we'll look at Chapter 3 and exactly how to shift your mindset to become happier and more charismatic.

Chapter 3 – Exactly How to Fix Your Mindset

"There's always room for improvement. That's my mindset."
Aaron Donald

What Is Mindset?

Mindset is the way you view the world. Your perceptions and biases create your mindset, and it is your mindset that determines how you react and respond to different situations. It is also your internalization of certain beliefs, with some of these beliefs becoming self-limiting. It's these beliefs that stop you from succeeding and appearing charismatic.

But what does mindset have to do with charisma?

– Everything!

You may feel like you're great at hiding your negative emotions and thoughts, but the chances are that they are flowing out into your body language and behaviors. A positive mindset is vital for charisma because when you speak or communicate with others, without realizing it, you broadcast messages about your mindset through your words and body language that they can pick up on. This is important because we are attracted to and captivated by positivity and success. Hence, people with the right mindset are naturally attractive to others and more likely to hold their attention.

The link between mindset and success is well established. So, it's not surprising that considering how charisma is linked to success, that mindset will be strongly linked to charisma.

How Mindset Influences Charisma

There's more to your personality than your outward traits. Your mindset is a big part of who you are and how others perceive you. A positive mindset is crucial for better charisma because anything less can prevent you from being perceived as charismatic.

People with a positive mindset are naturally charismatic and inspiring. When they speak, people listen. Charismatic people are often described as 'magnetic,' and their positivity gives them alluring qualities that so many are instantly drawn to.

Negative people, on the other hand, are draining to be around. After spending time with someone negative, you will often feel physically and mentally drained and a little more pessimistic yourself.

However, positive people have an infectious energy. They can make you feel lifted and positive after spending time with them. Naturally, it's the positivity that we are drawn to the most because we get a boost just by being around these types of people. Charismatic people always have a positive mindset. It's almost impossible to be charismatic if you're a negative person or always expecting the worst.

You Get What You Expect

Your mindset often determines the opportunities presented to you. When attuned to negative thinking, you see and attract negativity. Repeatedly using negative thinking patterns will wire your brain to respond accordingly by looking for confirmation bias in every situation. If, however, you've trained your brain to seek positives, it will find them for you. Now the confirmation bias is working in your favor.

When looking to change your mindset, the best place to start is with your words – and in particular, the words you use towards and about yourself. If you're always telling yourself negative things about who you are – shy, awkward, not good at something, then that is essentially what you will be. You internalize those words as beliefs, and unconsciously you are making sure that your behaviors match the expectation that you hold about yourself.

The words you use about yourself to other people are also important. If you tell people negative things about yourself and are constantly self-deprecating, they will start to accept what you say about yourself and begin to look for evidence to support it as the truth. Even though they would not have seen you in this negative light otherwise. On the other hand, saying mostly positive things about yourself will suggest that others associate these positive things with you.

Your words are powerful. That's one of the reasons that affirmations are so popular. It's not a magical incantation, but it works for resetting your mindset because you are sending your brain a particular message by feeding it more positive words. Over time this can rewire your thinking patterns and how you perceive yourself.

Make a habit of noticing the words you use about yourself. When they are negative, try and replace them with something positive. The words you replace them with must be something you believe to be true. For example, if you tell yourself, 'I'm not charismatic,' then saying to yourself that you are isn't going to be believable. Instead, say, 'I'm studying and practicing the skills that will make me more charismatic.' Or 'my charisma level is improving all the time.'

Mindset Changing Exercises

Changing your mindset requires a little bit of work, but the results are worth it. Here's a collection of exercises to help you shift a negative mindset into a positive one; one that will make you naturally more charismatic.

Affirmations

Affirmations are positive statements that can help you overcome negative thoughts about yourself. They're also one of the simplest exercises to incorporate into your routine. Make time to repeat you're positive affirmations daily, ideally more than once. When you wake up and before you go to sleep are great times to choose. But any time is fine as long as you can be consistent with it.

Affirmations need to become a habit to succeed. Consider them as essential for your brain as physical exercise is for your body. They work very well, but you have to commit to doing them and be consistent to see any real change. If you can commit to doing them regularly, you will see a big change in the way you think about yourself over time.

It's best to write your own affirmations, as they will resonate better with you by feeling more authentic.

However, here are some sample affirmations that you can tailor as you wish:
- I am a good listener.
- I focus on people when they are speaking, and I listen attentively.
- I am confident and can charm.
- People are drawn to my personality.
- Even if I am nervous, I can control my emotions and reactions.
- I am a great conversationalist.
- People listen when I talk.
- I can talk to anyone.
- I am confident and poised in all social situations.

Meditations
Meditating is an incredible habit to build. It's good for physical health, mental health, and it's also closely linked with success.

Like affirmations, meditation is something that needs to be done regularly and consistently to see the benefit. There are different kinds of meditations, and they can be as short as five minutes, so there's no excuse not to build one into your daily routine.

Meditation helps with charisma in several ways. Firstly, it helps you concentrate your focus and zone out distractions. This makes it easier for you to give people speaking to your full attention and be present in the moment. Secondly, it helps you stay calm in stressful situations, which is another key attribute that charismatic people have.

When we think of meditation, we often think of the person sat cross-legged on the floor, focusing on their breathing. While this is a very effective type of meditation, there are many other different types that you can try.

For beginners to meditation, guided meditations are usually the best choice. These are meditations that are led by someone else – often via an app or a recording. Many guided meditation apps are free and offer several different meditations to see what works best for you.

If you don't want to download an app, here are some simple meditations to try:

Focus on the breath – This is a very common form of simple meditation. You focus on your breath moving in and out of your body. If your mind wanders, you gently return it to focus on the breath.

Float your thoughts – This meditation involves simply sitting and clearing your mind of all thoughts. Because you're not focusing on anything, your mind is empty. Of course, thoughts will enter your mind, but you let them float away without paying attention to or acknowledging them.

Visualization – With visualization meditations, you imagine something so clearly that it seems real. When working on charisma, a good option is to visualize a situation where you are incredibly charismatic. Imagine every little detail of the environment, what you are wearing, how you feel, what you say. Make it as vivid as possible.

Reflective meditation – This type of meditation is good to explore your mindset. You reflect on a situation or a question, such as a work meeting, a social interaction, or why you find a certain charisma skill difficult. This is a fairly advanced form of meditation that requires a good degree of self-awareness and the objective ability to analyze your question without resorting to negative self-talk.

Creating A Meditation Space
The right environment can make a big difference in how successful your meditation is. Here are a few tips for getting the most out of your meditation session.

Find a quiet space where you know that you won't be disturbed or feel self-conscious.
Sit comfortably on a chair or cushion so that you aren't distracted by any physical discomfort.
Try and find somewhere to meditate that has natural light. Alternatively, candlelight can also create the right ambiance.
Switch off your phone and turn off any devices. Meditation is not a time for distractions.

Essentially, meditation is quite simple. Don't worry if your thoughts tend to still wander at first during meditation. Gently guide them back to where your focus needs to be. In time, you will become better at focusing your thoughts.

Journaling
Journaling is an excellent way to explore and improve your mindset. Your journal is a safe space where you can write down anything you want without fear of being judged. Journaling is perfect for uncovering your negative self-beliefs and examining why you think a certain way. This level of understanding is essential for taking action to improve how you see yourself and the world.

When journaling, you need to be honest about exploring your thoughts and emotions. It's a time for reflecting on how you handled certain situations, what went well, what didn't go well, and how you do things even better in the future.

Like meditation, it needs a quiet, comfortable space where you can relax. Turn off your phone and the television and concentrate completely on your thoughts, emotions, and what you want to write. It can feel strange at first but don't think too hard about what you're writing. If you're struggling to start, write down what you've done that day and then explore how you felt at various points and what might have been driving that feeling.

For example, you might write about attending a work meeting where you felt you didn't put your opinions across well enough. Why didn't you? Was it fear of something? What is behind that fear? The more you practice journaling, the easier it becomes, and the more easily you can identify and analyze your thoughts and emotions.

If you're still struggling to write freely, concentrate on how you feel now and write about that. Do you have any worries playing on your mind? Or any things you're feeling terrific about? Why are those things making you feel that way?

Once you've identified your thoughts and emotions in your journal, you can see how you might adjust your thinking to get a better outcome or how you can solve a particular problem or achieve more of a positive feeling.

Gratitude

Gratitude is a simple but powerful tool to adjust your mindset to a more positive one. By taking the time to think about the things you are grateful for consciously, you are drawing your attention to your life's positives – big and small. The more you practice gratitude, the easier you will find these positives in your life, which naturally makes you feel more positive in general. In as little as eight weeks, regularly practicing gratitude can help you become more positive by rewiring your brain to spot positives everywhere.

Gratitude is easy – make a conscious effort to notice the things you feel grateful for. They can be as small as a hot cup of coffee or as big as your spouse or children. You can work a gratitude practice into your journaling – take an extra few minutes at the end of your normal journaling to think of the things you are truly grateful for and write them down. You can also keep a separate gratitude journal if you prefer.

Gratitude is also a potent tool for enhancing charisma because you can use it to make people feel noticed. If someone has done something that made you feel grateful, tell them.

Vision Boards

Vision boards are often used to achieve material goals, but they can help you with self-improvement. The idea behind a vision board is that it's a visual reminder of what you want to achieve to keep you on track.

To create a charisma vision board, think about the end goals of why you want to become more charismatic. Seek out images or small items to attach to the board that represents the end goal. You can also add pictures of people you feel are charismatic that you want to emulate.

Real Life Case Study – Maria

Maria accepted a new job as a department manager, which meant she would be required to regularly deliver presentations to her department. Although she was highly qualified for the role, Maria struggled with public speaking, and as an introvert, she found that element of her role very challenging and stressful.

After the first few presentations being incredibly difficult, Maria decided that she needed to find ways to improve her presenting skills and become more confident when standing up in front of people. She had already attended courses on public speaking and presenting but felt that these weren't getting to the root of the problem.

Eventually, she stumbled upon an article about charisma – and decided that developing charisma might be the key to improving her presentation skills. Her charisma study led her to the concept of mindset and how negative self-beliefs can hold you back from effecting positive change.

Through meditation and journaling, Maria uncovered that a lot of her 'failure' at presenting was down to her own strongly-held belief that she just 'wasn't good' at it. Adding in affirmations to change that perception allowed her to change the way she approached delivering presentations.

Meditation also allowed her to feel less stressed and much calmer about delivering presentations. Using these powerful mindset tools, Maria delivered presentations in a much more confident manner, and she began to receive praise from her employees and line manager on how much more engaging the presentations had become.

We've already discussed how you can make people feel through your use of words, body language, and facial expressions. You now know it's these factors that determine how others will perceive you and if they will find you charismatic. Communication skills form another large part of being perceived as charismatic. In Chapter 4, we'll look at communication skills in further detail.

Chapter 4 – Communication Skills

"Take advantage of every opportunity to practice your communication skills so that when important occasions arise, you will have the gift, the style, the sharpness, the clarity, and the emotions to affect other people."
Jim Rohn

Assertive Communication

Charismatic people are assertive communicators. Assertiveness means being able to communicate calmly and confidently, even during a disagreement. Sometimes assertiveness is confused with aggression, but that's not the case at all. Being assertive is simply a matter of getting your point across in an exact, honest, and appropriate way.

Being assertive offers many benefits that go beyond being charismatic. Communication skills are essential for success, and assertive communication is the most effective communication style there is.

Assertive people can effectively express their feelings in a way that others can easily understand. And when others are clear about your needs, they are more likely to consider and meet them.
Assertive people are also likely to enjoy better personal relationships because they are open and honest and listen carefully to others' concerns and opinions without

dismissing them.

Assertiveness is a skill that anyone can learn, which allows you to communicate better and be more charismatic. You can learn to be assertive in the same way you learn any new skill - study and practice.

Here are some of the critical components of communicating assertively:

Don't try to control other people. Assertive people know that they can't control others' behavior; they can only control their own. By being self-aware and keeping reactions and emotions in check, assertive people become better influencers and persuaders – a key component of being charismatic. They make their position clear and then let the other person choose how to react to that information without making them feel railroaded.

Be honest, but avoid blaming. Charismatic people don't blame others for how they feel. Instead of saying 'you did this…' they will use 'I' statements. For example, 'I was disappointed when I was still waiting twenty minutes after the meeting time we scheduled.'

Using 'I' statements helps you avoid laying blame, making it easier for the other person to explain and or apologize without feeling attacked. Using I-statements usually means that others will respond more calmly, disagreements get resolved faster, and your positive relationship with that person stays intact.

Actively listen. Charisma is more about how you make others feel than it is about being loud, funny, or anything else. The best way to make people feel special? – Listen to them.

When someone is speaking, please give them your full, undivided attention. Let them talk without interruptions, and don't allow yourself to get distracted either by outside influences or forming a reply inside your head. When the other person finishes speaking, paraphrase back to them the key points of what they've just said so that they know you were listening. At this point, avoid giving advice or talking about yourself in any way. Just make it clear that you heard everything before you offer advice of any kind.

For example, when your friend is complaining about her boss piling the work on, listen carefully. When she's finished, you could say something like, "Sounds like your boss is putting the pressure on you without any reward or recognition, and that's making you feel pretty frustrated right now."

Bow out of disagreements gracefully. Charismatic people are persuasive, but they're not obsessed with winning every argument or talking around everybody to their point of view. If people disagree with your suggestions and opinions and aren't changing theirs, it's essential to agree to disagree and respectfully close the conversation.

Other Communication Styles

There are three other communication styles: Passive, Aggressive, and Passive-Aggressive. Understanding these different communication styles can help you recognize when you may need to change how you communicate to connect in a more charismatic way with your audience.

So, let's look at these in more depth:

Passive

Passive communicators tend to be quiet, shy, and reluctant to say no or enter into any confrontation. They will avoid eye contact and are often easily persuaded to change their opinion because they are uncomfortable with openly opposing others.

Suppose you're dealing with a passive communicator. In that case, listening is probably the most important thing you can do, closely followed by not reacting in an openly hostile manner to what they say. Other, more aggressive communicators often steamroll passive people–and so by taking the time to listen to them and make them feel valued, you will gain their respect.

Aggressive

Aggressive communicators aren't hard to spot. They're often loud, have expressive body language using gesturing and pointing, and aim to control the conversation as much as possible. Because aggressive communicators like to be heard, actively listening to them and summarizing their words back helps you gain their trust and respect.

Aggressive communicators like to 'win' every discussion, so it can be tricky when you're not in agreement. Look for points where you agree and work from there, but don't allow yourself to be steamrolled. Remember–gracefully bowing out is sometimes the right move.

Passive-Aggressive

Passive-aggressive communicators can initially look like passive communicators. Instead of ignoring or creating confrontation, they will subtly feed it and 'act out' if they feel they are being taken advantage of, but usually in hidden or underhanded ways. They can give the impression of being co-operative to your face but later actively be obstructive out of your view or hearing. In a mild situation, they might indicate their disagreement or disapproval with sarcasm or jokes.

Passive-aggressive communicators also want someone to listen to them and acknowledge their opinions.

Body Language

According to a study done in the 1960s, communication is 7 percent verbal, 38 percent vocal, and 55 percent visual. And in the modern world, where video calls are replacing telephone calls at a rapid pace, it's more important than ever to be aware of the visual signals you are giving out and to be able to read the signals others are sending to you accurately.

Body language is vital. When your words and tone of voice deliver one message, the signals you send via body language can send an entirely different message. Making sure that all of your verbal and non-verbal communication is aligned will help others read you as authentic – and more charismatic.

Another advantage of understanding body language is that being aware of body language signals from others can allow you to pick up on issues or bad feelings that they aren't verbalizing. Gestures help you identify whether others perceive the message you are delivering to them positively or negatively.

<u>**What signals are you sending?**</u>
We'll cover body language in much greater detail in Chapter 7. However, let's take a brief look at some prevalent 'negative' signals that you might be sending out unconsciously to others that can damage your charisma.

Eye contact. Too much eye contact can make you come across as aggressive, whereas too little can make you seem shy – or even untrustworthy.

Fidgeting makes you seem nervous. If you have a habit of pen-clicking, foot-tapping, or any restless, repetitive behavior, try to be aware of this and stop doing it.

Posture. Slumped shoulders or a downward-tilted head can send out signals of nervousness, boredom, or discomfort.

Distance. Standing too close or too far away from people can send out the wrong signal. Too close will make people feel uncomfortable; too far away can make you seem emotionally and physically distant and make it harder to hear each other.

Facial expressions. Most people think they control their facial expressions well, but they don't, and expressions are among the most significant accidental indicators you can send out. Try to keep your expressions relaxed. A clenched jaw, furrowed brow, or raised eyebrow can send out the wrong signals to others.

Active Listening

Active listening is a more effective way of listening. That might sound odd – indeed, listening is automatic, not a skill, right? But research suggests that we only remember between 25 percent and 50 percent of what we hear – the average person is only paying attention to less than half of the conversation.

That's why people who are excellent listeners are so valuable and well-liked. They're incredibly rare.

One of the reasons we don't listen with 100% of our attention is that we evolved to be constantly filtering stimuli around us to assess for dangers. So, we're hard-wired not to give our full attention to anything that doesn't represent a threat. Luckily, there are ways to improve your focus and train yourself to listen more attentively.

By becoming a better listener, you can improve your productivity, as well as your charismatic ability to influence, persuade, and negotiate.

Active listening involves making a conscious effort to hear not only the words that another person is saying but, more importantly, the complete message. Active listeners not only listen to what's being said, but they also pick up on the communication style of the message. They are great at reading between the lines of a conversation because they pick up on all the verbal and non-verbal signals that help you to understand the whole message the speaker is trying to convey.

The first step to listening more actively is learning how to focus your attention and avoid becoming distracted. Concentrate on what the other person is saying. If you find your mind wandering, bring it back to the present moment by focusing briefly on your breathing. Another trick is to momentarily pay attention to the feeling in your fingers or toes.

When you're able to focus on what the other person is saying, avoid trying to develop responses while they're speaking. Please give them your full, undivided attention and hear everything they have to say.

The second step to listening more consciously is to be aware of your body language. People are continually reading signals you send out – whether they do this consciously or subconsciously. Make appropriate eye contact and keep your body language open. Folded arms, hunched shoulders, or a negative facial expression can make you seem disinterested or as though you are going to react negatively to their message.

Relaxed your shoulders, tilt your chin very slightly up, and place your arms with wrists facing the person you are speaking to. All of these can help you come across as open to listening and receiving, and understanding a message correctly. Give small gestures as the other person speaks, such as nodding gently and smiling where appropriate. Never interrupt. Let the speaker finish what they are saying and watch for their cues for you to speak. Depending on what they are saying, you should either paraphrase or ask a relevant question to show you were listening.

For example, earlier in this chapter, I mentioned that if your friend complained about her boss, you could summarize her key points and how she had said what impacted her emotionally. However, you could also ask a relevant question here, such as, *"Is this a recent development,"* or, *"Does your boss treat anyone else like that?"* Of course, you should ensure that you don't ask a question that the person has already provided the answer to, as it will have the opposite effect entirely! There's nothing that loses people's trust and confidence in your listening skills more than making them repeat themselves.

Most of us have experienced the awkward situation of being involved in a conversation where you weren't sure if the other person was listening to what you were saying. It makes you feel unsure they understand you or even if it is worthwhile continuing speaking. It can also negatively affect your self-esteem by making you feel less than worthy of their attention. Chances are you're unlikely to think of the 'listener' as charismatic after an experience like that. It feels like talking to a brick wall, and it's something you want to avoid, so make sure you actively listen to people.

Please don't get too caught up in following all of the active listening actions; work on making one at a time feel natural to you and turn it into a habit. Focusing on too many at once is counterproductive. It can make active listening feel like you're crossing items off a checklist – and then you'll be focusing on the list and not listening.

If you struggle to keep focus, try practicing mindfulness separately every day. For five to ten minutes when you're alone. For example, with your morning coffee, focus entirely on the coffee. How it tastes, the smell, the warmth on your hands from the cup, and so on. Focus is a lot like a muscle – you can train it. However, in today's frantic world, where people check their devices every few seconds and try to multitask constantly, it's harder than ever to focus on one thing, so it will take dedicated practice.

When you've mastered the basics of active listening, here are some additional tips to help you take it to the next level:

Practice a pleasantly neutral facial expression.
Sometimes, when actively listening, people will assume that you agree with what they are saying. While it's true that actively listening involves being open-minded, there are going to be times you don't agree, and being an assertive communicator means being able to disagree confidently.

Select the right environment. If you know a conversation is going to occur, try to select a venue that helps you focus. For example, trying to actively listen in a crowded bar with loud music playing will be difficult. Sit with your back to apparent distractions, like large windows where people are walking past, televisions, or any other visual stimulus that could distract you. Try to avoid music, especially if you have to speak louder to be heard over it. And wear comfortable clothing to prevent any of the distraction and discomfort that can come from wanting to adjust your clothing.

Handle emotions. Sometimes you are going to have a strong emotional reaction to what's said. If this is the case, try to stay calm, clarify, and explain to the person speaking how you are feeling. For example, *"Can I check what you mean when you say that you don't think I'm a good friend? Is there something in particular that makes you feel that way because I feel that I have supported you in X, Y, and Z in the past?"* In all cases, if you're not sure, ask for clarification. People don't like repeating themselves, but if you can summarize their words to show that you were listening and ask for clarity, they will usually be happy to expand.

Always treat the other person respectfully, regardless of how you feel about what they have said. Responding negatively rarely makes you feel better or resolve anything.

Real Life Case Study of Charismatic Communication

Lois started a new job working for a large consultancy firm as an administration manager. Her new team was long-serving staff members, and not all of them were receptive to change or happy about an external candidate been put into the role. In her first week on the job, there was an uneasy atmosphere to the team, and Lois could feel that it affected their productivity.

Lois knew that to win them over quickly and become an effective manager, she'd need to be as charismatic as possible – starting with assertive communication. In her first week, she scheduled a meeting with each staff member individually to get to know them and understand their career goals and how they saw the team's future.

She set up the meeting room so that there were no distractions, ensuring she would focus entirely on each team member. Although she brought a notepad and pen with her, she didn't touch them until the person had finished speaking during each meeting. Once each person had finished, she paraphrased or asked questions to clarify before making any notes.

When addressing any concerns raised by her new team members, Lois took care to remain calm, non-judgmental, and keep her body language open. When tackling any confrontational statements, she remained calm. She used non-blaming language through the use of 'I' statements to clarify or explain her position without shying away from discussing the difficult topics.

By the time all of the meetings had taken place, she had greatly improved the atmosphere and relationship with many staff members.

Effective communication is a critical skill to have, and it can help you in any situation. It's not only crucial in a workplace setting; it can help you resolve personal conflicts, develop better personal relationships and help to explain your feelings and emotions clearly so that other people can meet your needs. Oh, and yeah, it helps with improved charisma too ;).

Chapter 5 – How To Talk To ANYONE

"A real conversation always contains an invitation. You are inviting another person to reveal herself or himself to you, to tell you who they are or what they want."
David Whyte

Communicating With Family & Friends

It might sound strange to have a section devoted to how to communicate with family and friends. Surely these are the people you should communicate best with?

Unfortunately, many people struggle to communicate effectively with the people closest to them. Combine this with the added pressure of working on your self-improvement, and many fear that their close family and friends will judge them for trying to become something they are not. Often, when we try to improve ourselves, one thing that holds us back is that people who know us best will disapprove of or not give their support.

At the start, it may feel bizarre and inauthentic, changing how you communicate with and behave around people who have known you for most of your life. Yet, communicating more assertively with those closest to you doesn't mean changing completely.

Currently, the way you communicate with friends and family will be influenced by various factors, including your shared history and interests. Your communication will continue to be influenced by those things, but hopefully in a more meaningful and positive way.

The pitfalls of communicating assertively with friends and family

We often assume that communication with them should be fairly effortless because we have spent a lot of time with our friends and family members. These people know us extremely well, so we expect them to understand us. When they don't, it can make you feel annoyed or even sad. However, the fact remains that communicating with those we know very well can be the hardest type of communication.

We assume that we provide them with more information about ourselves than we would colleagues or strangers because we communicate with them frequently. But as you know, most people are not great listeners and only take in about 50% of what we say. So often, when we think we've communicated a message, it hasn't actually been heard and understood.

Add to this the assumptions about our shared knowledge from living in close quarters, and we often make the mistake that they will understand the context of the situation or discussion, when in fact, they don't.

You can also fall into the trap of expecting close friends and family to pick up on your subtle moods and messages. For example, your sarcasm might be interpreted as sincerity or the other way round. Or we may think we are sending a signal that we need help or assistance with something, but they don't seem to pick up on that message.

This is where active listening can help you avoid being the person who misunderstands or doesn't pick up a subtle message. By listening carefully and asking for more information when you need it, you can easily get to the bottom of what someone is really trying to tell you.

Conversely, you can use some of the same skills to reinforce your message with the other person by subtly checking their understanding of what you've just said. By asking them what they think about a situation or their preferences on something, it focuses their attention and can highlight any gaps in their understanding.

It's imperative to do this in emotional conversations because people often create their understanding of messages by filtering it through the lens of how they feel at the time. So saying to your spouse, *"don't worry about it, I'll do it,"* could be interpreted as you being helpful or you being frustrated with them – depending on both your non-verbal signals and their own emotions at the time.

Generating Impactful Personal Conversations

Many of the conversations you have with your nearest and dearest won't need to be impactful. Sometimes they will be playful or just a way to let off some steam and have a good chat. However, when you're close to people, there will inevitably be times when you want to have serious conversations. Whether they are positive or negative, it's important to handle them properly to make sure that everyone understands your message correctly.

The first thing to consider is location. For example, broaching the topic of having another child with your spouse is probably something best done in a calm, relaxed, private environment, and not while shopping for groceries.

The other thing to consider – especially if there's a chance you won't agree on everything, is to make sure you aren't entering a discussion, having made several pre-judgments and assumptions. This is another area where active listening comes in really useful. Listen to the other person's reasons and opinions before persuading them into another way of thinking. Accept that they may not change their minds and find a middle ground if you can by really hearing what they have to say and looking for ways to meet their needs and your own.

Often, the person you are speaking to will surprise you. If you go in with an open mind, your body language and tone will put them at ease, and they may be much more receptive to what you have to say. And when you demonstrate active listening, they will be less likely to become defensive or to insist on their way purely on principle.

Another type of impactful conversation to have with friends and family is to get to know them better. You obviously already know them very well, but we can become a little blinkered about how people's lives, opinions, and needs are shifting over time. We expect people to stay static and familiar, but if you open up a conversation to understand them better, you may be surprised.

Try asking more open-ended questions of your family and friends – that go beyond, *"how was your day?."* Perhaps you could start by asking them what their favorite part of today was and why. Or if they've learned any new skills recently. You'll probably discover a lot about your nearest and dearest that you didn't know.

Talking To Strangers

As a child, you were probably taught the danger of talking to strangers – so it's no surprise that many adults find it daunting to speak to somebody they don't know. Most of your friends will have been strangers to you at some point, but somehow this doesn't seem to help when you find yourself at a function surrounded by strangers and need to pluck up the courage to start a conversation.

Often, the only problem is getting started. Once you manage to strike up a conversation, things flow naturally, and before you know it, you're chatting easily. Charismatic people can easily start conversations with strangers because they know that the stranger probably feels just as awkward as they do – and will likely be grateful that someone approached them!

How To *Actually* Make Small Talk

Small talk is basically just light, informal conversation. It's the obvious choice for starting a conversation with someone you just met, as you don't know what common ground you have yet. Here are some strategies to help you strike up a conversation with ease.

Look approachable – It's tempting to hide behind a device or distract yourself from your nerves with social media, but this will only make you look unapproachable to others. Nobody is likely to approach you with your phone in your hand, and it's even worse if you're distracted by your phone while trying to strike up a conversation.

Instead, put your shoulders back and smile, make eye contact, and look like somebody open to conversation.

Asking open-ended questions – gives people a chance to talk about themselves. Most people like talking about themselves, and using open questions ensures they don't let nerves get the better of them and give you a one-word answer.

The best questions encourage the other person to open up a little, although don't go in too soon with these, or you might come across as a bit too 'nosey.'

Use Active listening – We've mentioned active listening a lot in this book – but that's because it's such an important tool for putting other people at ease and coming across as charismatic. Active listening when talking to strangers has two big benefits. Firstly you'll pick up on more detail to ask further questions to keep the conversation going. Secondly, you'll come across as engaged with the conversation and put the other person at ease.

Simple Small Talk Topics
Having some prepared small talk topics will help put you at ease. Here are some topics that are good for almost any situation:

Your current location – An obvious topic of conversation is the location or environment you are in together. Is it a magnificent building or a trendy area? What's the local area like? Have you been before?

Local landmarks – You could discuss the local area if there are any specific famous or unusual landmarks. If they are local but you're not, or vice-versa, you could discuss some of the local landmarks' histories.

The weather – An obvious choice but a generally very safe one is to talk about the weather – particularly if it is or has been very warm, cold, or unusual weather that day. It's a good icebreaker, but make sure you have some other topics ready as it's usually exhausted quite quickly. A fun way to put a spin on the usual weather-related small talk is to ask what their favorite kind of weather is.

Travel – Most people have a good travel story, or at least a plan or a dream to travel somewhere exotic. A good way to open this one up is to ask if they have any travel recommendations for you or are going away anywhere nice soon?

Sports – Most people will have a sport they are interested in, and some people can happily talk about sport all day. Don't pretend to know something about a sport if you don't, and don't be embarrassed about that either. Chances are, if they're a sports fan, they will relish sharing their knowledge with you and educating you on one of their favorite topics.

Food – Like sports, most people will have a favorite food or type of cuisine and happily discuss it with you. And if you're really desperate, most people have a firm opinion on whether pineapple on pizza is a good thing or a bad one! You could also ask for restaurant recommendations or if they have any genius cooking tips for you.

Books and TV shows – Most people have a favorite book that they'll enjoy discussing. If not, they'll almost certainly have a favorite TV show.

Work – Another obvious one is to ask people what they do for a living. The key here is to listen and follow it up with good, open questions. Steer clear of generic questions like, "how long have you worked there?" and aim for thought-provoking ones that will generate conversation. For example, "what led you into that career" or "do you think this has been a good year, or a bad one for your industry?'"

Building Rapport

Asking the right questions and opening up a conversation is the hardest part of approaching strangers. However, if you're looking to make an impression on people, it's important to pay attention to developing rapport with them.

What Do We Mean By Rapport?
Rapport is the formation of a connection with somebody. Mostly it's the ability to relate to each other to encourage mutual trust and respect. When you build rapport with people, it's often the first step to friendship or a business relationship of some kind.

Some ways to develop rapport are:

Positive body language – Keep your body language positive at all times. Avoid folded arms or nervous gestures. Keep good, steady eye contact, and smile.

Mirroring – is a way of reflecting a person's body language at them. We do this unconsciously with many people we feel a close connection. By mimicking, you can make people feel more connected to you instantly. Of course, mirroring should be subtle and only mirror neutral or positive body language. Otherwise, you could generate the opposite effect! We'll cover more on body language in Chapter 7.

Talking To Colleagues, Clients, Or Superiors

The way you communicate in the workplace is often different from communicating with friends and family or strangers. The professional nature of work means a different approach is required – but the core charismatic skills of actively listening and remaining assertive stay the same.

Look For The Common Goal – A key part of most people's roles is to persuade and influence others. Whether it's persuading clients to buy your product or persuading team members to work towards targets, most people find that persuading and influencing is essential for success.

One way to approach conversations with clients and colleagues at all levels is to look for a common goal. How do your objectives and their objectives overlap? It may seem to be a straightforward question, but getting the answers requires you to use your charismatic communication skills.

Please don't assume you know what their goals are. You may have an excellent idea of the other person's goals and motivations, but don't assume that you know for sure. The best way to find out is to ask them and then listen to their response.

If you can find the overlap and leverage that, you can usually influence and persuade anybody to come around to your way of thinking. The key is to really listen to their objectives and develop your objection handling around those. This is much more effective than trying to force your way of thinking on them or making assumptions and trying to pre-emptively address concerns that they don't actually have.

Stay Friendly & Professional – Striking the right balance between friendly and professional can be difficult. If you come across as too friendly, you can lose trust. If you come across as too formal, you can lose rapport and engagement.

Charismatic people know how to keep the balance between professional and friendly just right. The key is to bring just enough of your natural personality into your workplace interactions while being mindful of the corporate culture.

Being friendly at work doesn't mean treating people like you treat your buddies. Just being open, honest, and respectful will go a long way towards making you seem warmer and more approachable without damaging your professional aura.

Handling Confrontation – Confrontation is unavoidable sometimes, but there are ways to handle it and come out on top without resorting to underhanded tactics or anything that could lose your trust or respect. Some key things to consider:

Be Diplomatic & Tactful – You never know what might be distasteful or offensive to another person, so avoid being flippant and remain respectful at all times. Humor can sometimes be great for defusing a situation but keep it light and appropriate. In a work environment, it's always better to err on the side of caution. If in doubt – don't say it.

Be Positive – Don't be unnecessarily negative. You can say you don't agree with something or think there's a better way to approach something – but be respectful and constructive about it.

Stay Calm – There's nothing less professional than losing your temper at work. If you're practicing assertive communication, this shouldn't be an issue. However, if you find yourself getting worked up, take some deep breaths, or make an excuse to get a glass of water or take a bathroom break to collect yourself. That way, you can return with a clearer head, ready to solve problems rather than create them.

Quickly Become Better at Written Communication

You're more likely to be using written communication to convey important messages in the workplace than anywhere else. While charisma is predominantly an in-person phenomenon, it pays to be mindful of keeping your written communications in line with your verbal communication.

It can undo all your hard work building your charisma if you send an email that sounds as though it's from a different person entirely.

It can help to consider your 'personal branding.' Companies use branding as a way to create an identity for their business. They choose a color scheme and logo that reflects the business, and the most successful businesses also develop a 'brand voice' that they stay true to in all forms of communication.

Here are a few things to consider when writing emails at work:

Tone – Aim for a conversational but professional tone. Don't use words and phrases that you wouldn't use in a face-to-face meeting or a telephone call. One way to achieve this is to dictate your emails. Most devices have a speech-to-text facility that can usually transcribe what you say very accurately. Just don't forget to edit your emails for correct spelling and proper grammar and punctuation to retain a professional image.

Be mindful that written communication is very susceptible to being misinterpreted when it comes to tone. With no metacommunication (non-verbal cues) to help them decipher it, the recipient will usually filter the tone based on their current mood and their past experiences with you.

Signoff – How you sign off your emails can make a big difference in how the recipient perceives the overall tone and message. 'Sincerely' can seem a little too formal, and 'Thanks' can seem a little too brief. 'Best wishes' is often a good choice as it's universally positive and unlikely to be misinterpreted. Don't forget the golden rule, though – stick to using a language you would use naturally. Don't sign off in a way that is completely unnatural for you.

Consider if a phone call is better – Sometimes, it's just too difficult to put something in an email in a way that gets your message across clearly and with the right tone. When it's just not working, don't be afraid to pick up the phone and have a conversation – it could avoid unnecessary misunderstandings.

General Tips

Metacommunication – We've talked about non-verbal signals like body language, facial expressions, and tone in Chapter 4. One term for these signals is metacommunication. These are the small signals we send out every day that enhances or skews the message's information.

For example, that look you exchange with your best friend that tells each other you find something funny, but it wouldn't be appropriate to laugh. Or the gesture you use to let your spouse know not to say something to the children. Or a simple nod of thanks to a stranger that holds open a door. There are dozens of examples of metacommunication that you participate in daily that you probably don't even think about.

Understanding what another person is saying to you means trying to understand all of their metacommunications as well.

First Impressions Matter – While charisma isn't really about your appearance, it's important to remember that many people will make judgments about you based on how you appear to them. They may not be correct assumptions, but understanding how to present yourself in a way that minimizes negative judgments when needed can help you stay one step ahead.

It's commonly known that a hiring manager often decides if a person is suitable for a job in the first few minutes of an interview. First impressions aren't just about what you wear, however. They're also about the metacommunication that you're displaying. Your posture, gestures, tone of voice. These can all impact a person's first impression of you.

First impressions are often surprisingly accurate. Several studies have been completed demonstrating that people can often judge a person based only on a photograph.

But how do we make such fast judgments about people?

It's all linked to our reptilian brain. The most primitive part of our brain, our reptilian brain, exists to keep us safe from danger. Milennia ago, our cavemen ancestors would have needed to make split-second judgments about whether another human or animal was a threat. Making the wrong judgment could be fatal. As a result, we developed an uncanny ability to use non-verbal clues to identify friend from foe in a concise space of time.

If you can make a positive first impression, you've immediately given yourself a charisma advantage.

Positivity – People are naturally drawn to other positive people. Being around a negative person for too long can be draining, and we don't tend to consider people we find to be negative as being charismatic.

Being positive doesn't mean you have to pretend to like things that you don't or be a 'yes' person all of the time. A quick reframe of a situation is usually all it takes to create an entirely different impression and come across as more charismatic.

For example, instead of saying, *"I don't like pizza,"* when choosing somewhere to eat, you could say, *"I love Chinese or Thai food – do you like those?"* Or instead of saying, *"That work wasn't up to standard,"* you could say, *"Let's discuss a few ways to improve this report."*

Now that we've looked at communication and striking up conversations in more detail, let's move on and explore the personality traits associated with being charismatic – and how to develop them.

Chapter 6 – The Charisma Guide…It's Easier Than You Think

"Personality is essential. It is in every work of art. When someone walks on stage for a performance and has charisma, everyone is convinced that he has personality. I find that charisma is merely a form of showmanship. Movie stars usually have it. A politician has to have it."
Lukas Foss

Being charismatic involves more than just effective communication. It also requires you to display several positive character traits. This is probably one of the reasons many people feel you are either born charismatic or not. Luckily, you can develop character traits just like you develop any skill.

You may have some natural propensity for certain traits either because of your innate personality or upbringing and learned behaviors. However, you can amend, adapt, and change these with conscious effort if you want to do so.

Patience

Patience is the ability to tolerate delays and frustrations without becoming angry, anxious, or upset. Patient people control their emotions and impulses in the face of difficult or frustrating situations. This is an essential trait for practicing assertive communication and active listening, as discussed in Chapter 4.

Without the patience to calmly sit and listen to another person, you can't master active listening. Without the patience to work through emotions and respond calmly, you can't communicate assertively.

There are other benefits to developing patience:

Lower stress levels – Patient people control their emotions and can wait to see how situations play out without becoming upset and angry.

Can see the 'big-picture' – Patient people have the ability to focus on a longer-term picture without needing instant results. It seems like everywhere you look, someone promises you solutions to all your problems in a short timeframe. *'Lose 10lbs in 10 days!' 'Learn a language in a month!'* and so on.

And while some people might see success in programs like this, most people don't achieve great results. Lots of things in life need patience. Losing weight healthily takes time. Learning to be fluent in a language takes time. Developing your charisma takes time.

Patient people learn to appreciate – they see the learning journey as important as the outcome, and they keep pushing towards their goals.

Patient people make better decisions – because they know the value of taking a little time to weigh up the pros and cons and gather all the information to assess it.

However, patience is difficult to master, especially in a world accustomed to instant gratification for most things. Here are some ways you can develop your patience:

Meditate – Meditation has various proven health benefits, including lower blood pressure and better mental health. It also teaches patience and focus, two key skills for developing charisma.

Reflect – Reflecting at the end of each day where being more patient would have been helpful and where you managed to be patient that day
can help you recognize your need for patience in future situations. Choose to spend a little time each day being conscious about patience.

Slow down and take your time – When completing a task or having a conversation. See how it changes the outcome.

Choose to think before you speak – Take one deep breath before saying anything; give yourself time to think and assess if what you are saying is helpful, necessary, and truly communicates your message.

Tolerance

Closely linked to patience, tolerance is the ability to accept other people and situations that we perhaps don't like for what they are, while at the same time accepting that we can't change them.

It's easy to think about your tolerance – or lack of it – in terms of other people. *"If she wasn't so loud…" "He should have better manners,"* and so on. However, your tolerance is nothing to do with anyone else and everything to do with you. It basically boils down to how you choose to perceive others.

To develop tolerance:

Stop blaming others and take responsibility – Remember that nobody makes you feel a certain way. Just as they can choose to behave one way, you can choose how you respond.

Identify why something or someone bothers you – Often, when we find someone annoying, the root of what causes that is within us. How we feel about that person says more about us than it does about them. Are they behaving in a way that you wouldn't allow yourself to behave? Are they preventing you from being heard or getting something you need?

When you discover the root of your annoyance, you can deal with it.

Whatever or whoever is annoying you, remember it is only temporary. Use your patience to wait it out without getting worked up or upset.

Exercise your power of choice – You choose how to respond or react to any situation or person. You also have the power to choose how strongly you feel about something.

Tolerance doesn't mean blindly accepting abusive or truly unacceptable behavior. Still, it does mean understanding why you find somebody or something irritating or offensive. You have the power to choose to react in the most positive and constructive way possible.

Respect

Respect is central to charisma. Charismatic people gain the respect of others, and they exhibit respect for other people. Crucially, they also respect themselves.

Active listening is an excellent way to demonstrate respect for someone. You can respect people without agreeing with them. Respect is about recognizing that their point of view is valid and that their opinion is just as important as any other person's.

Everybody deserves respect. Some people may gain more respect than others, but at a basic level, everybody deserves to feel like they have value, and that's what charismatic people deliver. They make you feel valued.

Self-respect is just as significant as having respect for others. To be charismatic, you need to be confident, at ease with yourself, and believe in your own worthiness before making others feel good about themselves. Self-respect isn't about being perfect; it's about recognizing and acknowledging what you do well and resolving to improve on the things that matter to you. And that you do this without beating yourself up about mistakes or shortfalls.

Trust

Trust is a fundamental element of any human interaction. It's imperative in personal relationships and management positions to build trust with others. But what is trust?

It's confidence in somebody's honesty, integrity, and

reliability.

Like respect, trust works both ways. You need to trust others as well as inspire trust in others. And people's trust can't just be gained instantly. However, you can start a relationship with increased trust levels by being open, honest, and aware of your body language. Good eye contact can help build trust, as people who are not truthful often find it difficult to maintain eye contact when lying.

Trust is cultivated and needs to be maintained with consistent demonstrations of honesty, integrity, and reliability. Maintaining trust is very important because it is much harder to regain trust than to lose it.

Some simple ways to build and keep trust:

Do what you say you will – If you can't do something, be open and honest upfront about it.

Keep people's confidence – If you don't think you can keep something confidential to yourself for reasons such as illegal activity or placing somebody in danger – be open and honest about that too.

Don't lie – People will trust and respect you more for telling the truth – even if it means admitting a mistake.

Admit mistakes – This takes confidence and vulnerability, but if people can see that you will admit when you have made a mistake, it builds their trust in your integrity.

Be Non-Judgmental

Judging others is something we often do without thinking much about it. We use our own experiences and values to make assumptions about someone's life or their worth. Yet judgment isn't only damaging for the person being judged. It's also keeping your mind narrow and potentially preventing you from taking advantage of opportunity.

Our tendency to judge probably has its roots in our tribal ancestry. For early man, 'different' could really mean dangerous, as rival tribes might fight over territory and resources. However, it doesn't help us much in today's society, where recognizing and celebrating differences helps us be healthier, happier, and more successful.

We've already discussed how respect is a vital part of being charismatic – and respect means not making snap decisions about people based on their looks, race, nationality, gender, or individual choices like fashion.

When we judge others, it's simply a reflection of how we see the world – not a reflection of reality. Not everybody holds the same values or strives for the same things. Success looks different to everybody, and so does beauty. And boy, oh boy, wouldn't it be a boring world if everyone was the same?

Beyond idealistic concepts, judgment stops us from listening properly to others. It creates a bias that makes us behave a certain way towards others based on your 'truth.' So, we might trust somebody who doesn't deserve it simply because we made assumptions based on superficial features and what those features mean to our truth. Or we might overlook the perfect candidate for a role because we thought they weren't dressed well enough for an interview.

The opposite of judgment is observation. Developing your

observational skills can help you stop judging others unnecessarily. It's unrealistic to say you will 'stop' judging other people – in some ways, it's part of our hard-wiring as humans. However, we have the ability to override it by being self-aware and recognizing when we're judging. Observe yourself making the judgment, acknowledge it for what it is – a bias and an opinion, not a fact. This way, you can choose to look beyond the judgment and gather the facts.

Over time, you will naturally judge a little less because your experience will have taught you that the man with tattoos up his neck, which you assumed was a thug, may actually be a family man who spends his spare time rescuing orphaned kittens.

Humor

Humor is a great trait to have to help you come across as more charismatic. Everybody likes a person who can make them laugh – why else would *'must have a good sense of humor'* be such a dating cliché? Even better, humor is a learned skill. Young children learn about humor as part of their language development – especially when it comes to wordplay.

So, if you don't consider yourself as somebody with a good sense of humor, you might be relieved to learn that you can develop it.

Or perhaps you have a well-developed sense of humor, but it leans towards the inappropriate or sarcastic. While many people may find it funny, it doesn't lend itself well to charisma. That kind of humor can be very divisive, and charismatic people tend to be more universally appealing with their type of humor.

The kind of humor that charismatic people possess is very good-natured and pleasant. They can accept a good-natured joke about themselves without being offended. They also don't find humor in others' misfortune or in things that most people would find distasteful – or if they do, it's certainly not something they display in public.

Laughter helps people feel good, and if you can generate that feeling in other people, you are naturally more magnetic to them. Humor can lighten a mood and even help get to the heart of difficult or sensitive matters.

Getting the balance right is important. Trying to make everything into a joke means that you will inevitably take it too far or become annoying rather than funny. Practical jokes are also something to avoid as they can have unintended consequences and often rely on making somebody else look stupid.

To keep your humor appropriate, try, and consider:
- Is it kind?
- Is this an appropriate place and time?
- Could it be offensive in any way?
- And if in doubt, don't tell the joke!

Honesty

Honesty is a precious trait that helps you build trust and respect with others. Most people believe they are honest, but if we really examine ourselves, we can all be more openly honest more of the time.

Honesty isn't just about the big things – not lying, cheating, stealing, and so forth. Often the lies we tell are small and seemingly innocent 'white' lies. We may even tell ourselves that they were for the greater good. Or we are dishonest by our choice of staying silent. We may not actually lie, but we don't provide the truth, either.

Other examples of dishonesty are saying yes to please others when we want to say no, and agreeing with something we don't really agree with, to avoid confrontation.

While it would be pleasingly simple to say that 100% honesty 100% of the time was the only acceptable answer, the reality is that it isn't always possible. If a child asks a difficult question about death or the existence of Santa, it may not be appropriate to be completely honest with them at that time. Or if someone asks what you're thinking, it might not always be the best idea to give them the full, uncensored detail.

Being as honest as you can be, for most of the time, should be your key aim – but don't fall into the trap of believing that you can be rude or offensive because it's 'honest.' Charismatic people are honest. Still, they're also diplomatic, tactful, and respectful.

Many of these traits share similar characteristics or have areas of overlap. Tolerance and respect are closely linked, as are honesty and trust. Developing one trait can often improve other traits naturally.

How to *Actually* Develop Charismatic Personality Traits

So, we've covered how to take steps towards cultivating positive traits, but how do you turn them into an ingrained personality trait, part of who you are?

By making them a habit.

The whole point of a habit is that it's consistent and regular behavior. Some habits are almost automatic, and building the right ones is crucial for success. The way we behave is mostly a series of habits that we've built over time. We build most of our habits unconsciously, but you can unlearn them and build new ones with conscious effort. And once you train yourself to think and respond a certain way, almost on auto-pilot, it makes it much easier to be genuinely charismatic.

How Do You Build Habits?

Motivation is the one thing people tend to think of when building new habits or breaking old ones. However, while motivation is great to get you started, it will eventually fade. That's why you need to apply a little self-discipline to bridge the gap between starting to build a habit and actually forming it into a habit.

When you build good habits, you no longer need to think about them. Things that took a lot of effort before, like actively listening, become second nature. Creating habits sets you up for success. A habit of daily meditation is a great place to start, as it supports many of the positive personality traits needed to be charismatic.

Aim to do some form of meditation every single day, no excuses, to condition your brain to understand that this is a habit. With enough repetition, it will become something you do daily and make time for – like brushing your teeth - instead of something you're just 'trying to fit in' to your day.

Making certain behaviors a habit can make it much easier to be effortlessly charismatic. So it makes sense to concentrate on building good behavioral habits – one at a time - that provide a cornerstone for your charismatic personality.

Developing Personality Traits into Habits

Forming a positive trait isn't always easy. Unlike bad habits that usually provide instant gratification like alcohol and smoking, good habits rarely give us that instant hit of self-gratification.

Don't be too hard on yourself if you struggle to build positive personality traits - we're hard-wired as humans to respond to instant gratification. It's that rush of dopamine that makes us want to keep repeating a habit, and positive habits rarely provide the same kind of gratification. They don't provide a hit of dopamine, so the reptilian part of our brains doesn't find them interesting enough to make us crave them.

However, with enough repetition, you can make any behavior a habit. There's no set number of days or repetitions to make something a fully-formed habit. It could take several weeks or several months before that happens.

This is why it's better to focus on developing one personality trait or breaking one old personality trait at a time. You might want to achieve permanent change faster than this – but remember, patience really is a virtue!

It's a reasonable expectation that it will take at least two months of conscious, daily repetition to build a habit. So, you're going to need some motivation and self-discipline to get you through this stage. The good news is, once the habit is built, it will be second nature.

Just remember that if you don't stay consistent, you're wiping out all your previous work for that personality trait, and you may have to start right back at square one!

Using Habit Triggers
One trick to building any habit faster is to use triggers. This is where you attach the habit to an event or action. Triggers can be anything–people, emotions, the time of day, a location, or any action we regularly do. It's anything at all that our mind associates with a habit.

You can use triggers to help build positive personality traits by linking the trait to a trigger. This helps and means you're more likely to maintain the change long-term. The more often you use a trigger to prompt a behavioral response, an action, the more ingrained it becomes until it's pretty much automatic.

Triggers are sometimes easier for physical habits than they are for developing personality traits, but they can work well—especially emotional triggers. If you find yourself becoming impatient, you can use that emotion as a trigger for the physical action of deep breathing, which will help you calm down, gain perspective, and develop patience. Locations can also be powerful triggers. When you associate a particular place strongly with a behavior, it's effortless to model that behavior in that location.

Chapter 7 – Charismatic Body Language

"Body language and tone of voice - not words - are our most powerful assessment tools."
Christopher Voss

Body language is imperative when it comes to communication and charisma. Whether they realize it or not, people read the non-verbal signals you send out via facial expressions, mannerisms, and general body language.

This means that it's almost impossible to be charismatic when your words and body language don't match. If your words are confident, but your body language is nervous, people will only pick up on the nerves. Your body language is an outward sign of your internal emotions, so monitoring and managing your own emotions and body language can help you control how others perceive you.

Of course, it's not just your own body language that you need to be aware of. Reading others' body language helps you understand how they perceive the message you are giving them – and the information to adapt accordingly. If you understand the signals people are giving you, you'll know when they're interested in what you have to say or when they think you're less than genuine.

Some people are natural body language readers, but it can be a learned skill that anyone can develop. In fact, one of the benefits of learning it as a skill is that you are more aware of your own body language as a result. Learning and practicing the tips and techniques in this chapter will help you apply body language knowledge to your own conversations and naturally improve your charisma.

The tips and advice given here are generic. Everybody will have subtle differences in their body language, depending on their culture, upbringing, and personal experiences. However, most people's body language will conform to some extent with the examples given here, so understanding these key elements of body language helps enhance charisma.

Observe The Body Language Of Charismatic People

The best way to learn about body language is to spot it for yourself. Make a point of observing charismatic people as they speak. Ted Talks videos are a great way to observe charismatic body language. But ensure you also watch out how charismatic people behave *'in the wild.'*

Try and identify some common body language signals that charismatic people display and choose one at a time to try and incorporate when you are speaking.

Here's a quick breakdown of common body language signals to look out for and what they are signaling to others.

Negative Body Language Signifiers
The following are all examples of body language signals that are likely to be perceived negatively by other people. Try and recognize when you are displaying negative body language and mindfully change it.

Understanding the negative signals also helps you in another way. Charismatic people are generally great at putting other people at ease. By recognizing signals that somebody may be feeling uncomfortable, irritable, or anxious, you can take steps to put them at ease.

Nervousness

Confidence is essential for being charismatic. If you want to project a more confident image, avoiding some of these common tell-tale signs of nerves can help. If someone you are speaking to is displaying these signs, a charismatic individual will make them feel more comfortable.

General fidgeting – For example, tapping a foot repeatedly, playing with an object, repeatedly clicking a biro.

Fidgeting with their clothing – For example, adjusting a tie, fiddling with a button, picking lint from clothing. This can signify that someone feels particularly nervous about their appearance, so a well-timed and genuine compliment can help put them at ease.

Clenched hands – This can indicate either negativity to what is being said or indicate anxiety more generally. Pay attention to the other signals and the context of a conversation to decide which is being displayed.

Erratic eye contact – If your eyes are darting around a lot, it will make you seem very nervous.

Perspiration – If someone is visibly perspiring and it's not very warm, they are potentially feeling quite nervous.

Arms folded, shoulders hunched – This is a defensive

stance, indicating that the person is subconsciously expecting an attack of some kind. The 'attack' could be verbal or just an unpleasant conversation.

Try and be aware of and correct any of these signals that you may be sending out. If someone else is displaying these signals, take suitable steps to put them at ease.

Dishonesty

The following signals indicate that somebody isn't completely honest with what they are saying. However, it could also be as straightforward as them not being their 100% authentic self or a little nervous. In any instance, try to avoid displaying them at all costs as appearing dishonest is an instant charisma killer.

Touching or covering your mouth or your nose during, or straight after, speaking – This could signify that the person is trying to stop themselves from saying anything more they shouldn't.

Hiding your hands – for example, placing them behind your back or in your pockets. Conversely, open palm gestures, and openly displaying the hands can be interpreted as a sign of honesty.

Frequently swallowing – If somebody's swallowing is very frequent, it could be a sign of lying.

Tugging at your collar – can indicate dishonesty. People tend to feel warmer or flushed when lying and this could be their attempt to get some cooler air.

Anger

These body language signals indicate that somebody is feeling angry and that the conversation may take a turn for the worse. Charismatic people are not aggressive, so avoid displaying these signals as they will always turn off your audience.

When you spot signals like these, you'll need to decide the best way to respond, depending on the situation. Often, charismatic people are excellent at defusing aggression and turning a situation around, but sometimes that isn't possible no matter how charismatic you are. Of course, aggression can be mild, or it can be more extreme, and you should always put your own safety above being perceived as charismatic.

Pointing – When people begin to get agitated about something while speaking, they may start to point or wag a finger.

Standing too close – This is often a way to try and make you feel intimidated. However, it can also be a sign of flirtation, although there would normally be other signals to indicate that.

Widened stance – People often stand with their feet wider and their hands on their hips when trying to appear intimidating. It's a subconscious gesture designed to make them appear larger and more threatening.

Wild hand gestures – These can indicate either high levels of excitement about a topic or anger/aggression.

Banging a fist on a surface – This is quite clearly an aggressive action and usually indicates someone feels particularly passionate about what they are speaking about and don't think others are listening properly.

When somebody becomes aggressive, most people will

respond in one of two ways. They will either respond with aggression themselves, or they will become nervous and withdraw from the interaction.

Handling aggression from somebody else is a tricky subject as the right response depends on many variables. However, when you understand the body language signals associated with aggression, you can take action more quickly. You'll be able to either calm the situation or remove yourself from it before it becomes outright hostile.

Boredom

Boredom is the last thing you want to see in someone's body language when communicating with them. Charismatic people engage their audience – regardless of size – they don't bore them. Luckily boredom is quite easy to spot in body language. If you see any of these signs, try and liven up what you are saying with an appropriate joke or consider if it might be time to stop talking.

The most obvious sign of boredom is looking away, out of a window, towards a door, or at a device – people may even look repeatedly at their clock as if willing the interaction to speed up and end.

Staring blankly – Almost the opposite of the former signal, someone who is bored might stare blankly. They're looking at you, but their mind is elsewhere.

Doing something else – Sending a text, talking to someone else, doodling. If they're focusing their attention elsewhere – you've already lost it.

Yawning and slouching – are commonly associated with boredom. They can be a reliable signal that you're boring your audience, but tiredness might not be linked to boredom with what you are saying.

If you spot signs of tiredness, consider the environment and the context you are in. Is it warm and stuffy? Is it just after lunch? If you can answer yes to both of those, then even the most charismatic person might struggle to hold attention. If possible, get your audience active to wake them up a little. Ideally, don't schedule meetings or presentations for after lunch and ensure the room isn't too warm or stuffy.

Disagreement
These body language signals indicate that somebody disagrees with what they are hearing or is critical of it. Being able to pick up on this means you will know when to change tack potentially or stop speaking and ask them what they think. That way, you can understand their point of view and make them feel listened to.

One or both arms crossed tightly over the body, hands resting on their upper arms just above the elbow, palms pressed down – indicates they want to protect themselves from what you might be saying.

Legs tightly crossed – In a similar manner to the arms-crossed gesture, if somebody has their legs crossed tightly, it can indicate that they disagree with what they are hearing.

Resting their elbows on the table, with clenched fists – When the hands are clenched tightly so that the knuckles are white, it's a clearer sign of negativity. However, this signal can also be anxiety, so take the context of the conversation into account.

Positive Body Language Signifiers

Confidence

These body language signals show that someone is feeling confident. These are the body language signals that you would expect to see from charismatic people.

Rubbing the palms together – When someone rubs their palms together, it may indicate excitement about the topic they are speaking about or that they expect a positive outcome to a particular matter.

Leaning forward when speaking – This tends to show interest and is usually done by the speaker to make the listeners feel as though something secret and interesting is being shared. Watch a charismatic person when they employ this signal, and you'll see that the audience will normally lean forward as well, mirroring the person.

Smiling – A true smile shows the teeth and affects the eyes – usually creating tiny wrinkles at the corners of the eyes and the eyebrows come slightly down. Closed-lipped smiles or smiles that don't affect the eyes are unlikely to be genuine or display confidence.

Good posture – with the shoulders back and relaxed and the chin parallel to the floor. This indicates that someone is comfortable in their own skin and feels that they belong. They aren't inviting attention, but they aren't trying to deflect it either. Adopting this posture is a quick way to appear instantly more confident.

Relaxed

These are body language signals that indicate someone is relaxed. These are good signals to recognize and understand because, ideally, you want to send these signals and see them in your audience.

Relax – Loosen muscles with no tension and relax shoulders down and back.

Hands open, palms facing upwards – We hide our palms when we are dishonest, or sometimes also when we are anxious or fearful. Displaying our palms to others means we are at ease and relaxed.

Good eye contact – When we are bored or anxious, we don't make good eye contact and tend to either look around the room or stare ahead without making eye contact. When we are relaxed, we can maintain appropriate eye contact.

Smiling – with a smile that touches the eyes and doesn't just move the mouth.

When people are relaxed, they're also more likely to be listening to you.

Agreement
Knowing when someone agrees can be a handy tool for persuasion – a key skill for being charismatic. The body language signals include:
- Head inclined slightly forward. Also, nodding is very obviously a sign of agreement.
- Hands open, palms visible. This also indicates honesty.
- Head tilted slightly to one side.
- Open posture, shoulders back.

Facial Expressions & Eye Contact

Facial expressions and eye signals are also body language, and they're potentially easier to spot than other kinds of body language. These are especially important in situations like video calling, where you might not get a full picture of someone's body language but can assess facial expressions instead.

Most of us know how to read facial expressions. We all know that a frown is a negative sign, and a smile is a positive one. Yet there are lots of other, subtler signals that we send with our facial expressions.

Here are some facial expressions and eye signals that convey particular emotions:

Smiling – A relaxed, genuine smile indicates someone is listening and interested in what is being said. In contrast, a tight-lipped smile or corners of the mouth drawn down can indicate that someone feels negative about what is being said or what they are saying. A tight-lipped smile can also indicate that someone is withholding information.

Corners of the mouth turned down – This can potentially indicate several negative emotions like unhappiness or anger, so pay close attention to the other signals being given.

Flared nostrils – This is the lizard brain preparing for fight or flight, allowing more oxygen in for the expected activity. Like sneering, it can indicate fear, anger, or irritation in humans.

Wide eyes – These can indicate surprise, shock, or anxiety. A sudden widening of the eyes tends to indicate shock, whereas if their eyes are generally wide and look away a lot, it could be nerves or anxiety.

Eyes darting around – This can indicate nerves if somebody is looking around constantly.

The Power Of A Handshake

A handshake can convey a lot of information about a person, and getting it right can boost your charisma potential immediately. A handshake is often the first physical contact you have with a person, and if it goes well, it is an opportunity to build trust – which, as we know, is essential to charisma.

Some common handshake mistakes to avoid are:

Limp handshake – A barely-there grasp and minimal movement of the hand can give the impression that you are timid, weak, or uninterested.

Dominating handshake – In contrast, a too-tight grip and overly robust movement can make you seem overpowering and domineering.

The overhand handshake – This is where you place your hand out, palm-down, and force the other person to accept your hand with their palm up. This is generally perceived as a power play.

Tips to get the handshake right:
- Keep your hand perpendicular – you should not tilt

your handshaking palm up or down.
- Keep your palm flat.
- Shake from the elbow, not the wrist.

Body Language *Combined* with Effective Speaking

Body language is just one element of charisma, but it is potent combined with effective communication. We covered a lot of charismatic communication in Chapter 4, but let's quickly recap some of the key points.

Charismatic people are assertive communicators. This means they are confident, articulate, and able to express themselves clearly without becoming aggressive or nervous. It also means that they actively listen when others are speaking, summarize back the key points to ensure that they have understood the message, and ensure the person speaking knows they have been listened to.

Your words, tone of voice, and body language must be all in sync. That way, you're sending the same message via verbal and non-verbal communication. This reassures your audience and makes you appear trustworthy and genuine.

Real Life Case Study – Janine

Janine was an efficient and competent employee, but she had been passed over for promotion on several occasions.

Although she was articulate and confident in a one-on-one setting, when it came to delivering presentations or sitting through an interview, Janine's introverted personality tendencies meant that although she knew exactly what to say, her non-verbal cues were completely unaligned with her words.

In a normal one-on-one work situation, Janine's body language was expressive and in line with her speech. Her colleagues found her to be warm, friendly, and charming. Unfortunately, she couldn't demonstrate any of these charismatic qualities in an interview or presentation, which was now holding her career back.

Janine knew that she had to tackle this problem to achieve the promotion she needed. So, she set to work on studying body language. She paid close attention when senior management members were delivering presentations, watching how they would stand and position themselves with the audience, how they would use hand gestures to emphasize their words, and how their posture exuded confidence.

She also began to study her own body language, paying attention to the natural gestures and posture she would adopt when relaxed and in familiar company. She began to be more aware of her non-verbal signals in meetings and informal workplace conversations, noting how people would respond when she adjusted her body language. For example, when she made a point of having her palms facing upwards when delivering a difficult message, she found the recipient would respond more positively than if she had her arms folded or palms hidden.

Janine was able to take this learning and use it in her next interview for a promotion. Despite feeling nervous, she ensured that she smiled, kept her shoulders back and chin parallel to the floor. When delivering her answers, she spoke at a steady and appropriate level. This time, she gained the promotion.

Paying attention to your body language pays off in a big-time to come across as more charismatic. Of course, body language is just one piece of the puzzle. It's only when your body language and message are fully aligned that you can truly come across as charismatic. But combined with the other sections of this book, body language is a handy tool to increase your charisma.

Paying attention to the body language of others is also useful. Chapter 1 discussed that charisma is about how you make other people feel and how you behave. Understanding body language cues allows you to identify if you're making people feel good – or not – and change how you communicate with them if their body language signals indicate negative emotions.

Charismatic communication isn't limited to the workplace, but most people want to be more charismatic to improve their career prospects. In the next chapter, we'll look at how to communicate charismatically at work.

Chapter 8 –
Communicating at Work

"Communication is a skill that you can learn. It's like riding a bicycle or typing. If you're willing to work at it, you can rapidly improve the quality of every part of your life."
Brian Tracy

We touched briefly on this in Chapter 4 but being perceived as charismatic in work means being mindful of how your colleagues and superiors perceive you, and if that doesn't match with how you want them to see you, you can take action to turn it around.

First impressions are important; we all know that. Starting a new job can be a wonderful chance to be the very best version of yourself and create great first impressions that starts you off on the right foot. Unfortunately, not everyone will be in that enviable situation. If you've worked in your company for any length of time, you will have already made first impressions and potentially had enough interaction with your colleagues that they have a fully formed opinion of you.

Hopefully, that opinion is a good one, and they find you at least a little bit charismatic. But if not, don't worry. First impressions are important, but it's possible to change how someone perceives you – it just takes more time and effort than achieving it on the first meeting.

Once you've created a great first impression, you get the benefit of confirmation bias. This is where that person will naturally think better of you and give you more leeway than if you didn't make a good first impression. Still, with consistent charismatic behavior, you can turn people's opinions around. However, you will need patience and consistency.

What's The Common Goal?

When dealing with colleagues and, in fact, when trying to resolve any situation at all – look for the common goal. What do both parties want to achieve? This is actually quite easy to do in the workplace, where colleagues' motivations tend to be job-driven. This is because you will already have some insight into the nature of their role in the company and what their own work objectives are likely to be.

If you can't easily identify the common thread, don't be afraid to ask outright. What is it that they need to achieve? What outcome or actions do they need from you or your department. Consider how these might align with your own goals? If they aren't aligned, is there a way to align them?

When you understand the common goal or at least the overlaps in your goals and interests, then you can much more easily persuade and influence others around to your way of thinking – and leave them feeling good about the interaction too. That's the power of charisma.

What's Your Role?

It's important to understand your role in any particular work project before you begin. If your role is to assess financial risk, but you are attempting to influence something beyond your role remit, it will be much harder to do than influence something well within your own remit.

If you're the office junior and you want to give the CEO

some ideas for improving the business, then it could go spectacularly wrong if you handle it in the wrong way.

That doesn't mean it's impossible to step outside of your box at work, but it does mean that you need a good understanding of the goals and motivations of those you're trying to influence and anyone that your desired outcome could affect. Done right, and with some really great ideas being put forward, stepping outside of your role remits could be the best career move you ever made.

If you are one hundred percent confident that what you are proposing is a sound idea and have relevant data or research to back it up, then using your charisma could be the difference between a hard 'no' and a resounding 'yes.'

Being Both Professional & Personable

In the workplace, there's often a lot of pressure to behave professionally. But what does that actually mean? Sometimes a need to remain professional is interpreted as a need to be super-formal and completely focused on work all of the time.

While good work focus is important, we're all human, not robots. It's your human side that draws people to you and fuels your charisma. So, while you don't want to throw too much caution to the wind and behave inappropriately, there's a lot to be gained from letting your personality shine through at work.

One way to do this is to indulge in inappropriate office

chit-chat. Getting involved in a little small talk with your colleagues can really boost your charisma. It gives you a chance to learn a little about their lives, empathize with them, and celebrate with them when appropriate. When you know a little about your colleagues, it's easier to demonstrate warmth towards them, and sometimes those small bits of information can prove invaluable when you're communicating in the 'boardroom' with them.
Understanding them better as people means that you can pitch your work based communication at the right level. It also means they get to know - and trust – you a little better, too.

Like everything in life, it all comes down to balance. Spending hours of your day gossiping at the water cooler isn't going to boost your charisma - the worst case could get you fired. Spending ten minutes or so asking a colleague how their weekend went or how their family is, however, can work wonders for office relationships.

Written Communication

Having your own 'brand voice' can help you to sound consistent across your written communication. It's not as contrived as it sounds; your 'brand voice' is your personality. People who know you will see fakeness if you are writing emails in a way that feels alien to you.
However, you'll want to be able to make certain elements of your personality stand out more than others. Thinking of your written communication as having a 'brand voice' that matches your 'in-real-life' personality can help make sure that you don't succumb to overly stiff and formal emails or memos that don't come across as charismatic at all.

Be mindful that texts, emails, letters, etc., are very susceptible to being misinterpreted when it comes to tone.

With zero body language, facial expressions, or pitch of the voice to help others decipher your message, the person receiving the written communication will usually filter the tone based on their current mood and /or past experiences with you.

How you sign off your emails can also make a big difference to the overall tone and message. 'Sincerely' can seem a little too formal, and 'Thanks' can seem a little too brief. 'Best wishes' is often a good choice as it's universally positive and unlikely to be misinterpreted.

Authenticity & Vulnerability

Charismatic people are authentic. They're genuine, and that shows. Don't confuse 'authentic' with 'natural' - they're related terms, but they're not the same. It doesn't mean that you can't develop charisma if you're not 'naturally' charismatic. It would be best to enhance the personality traits and habits that make you more charismatic and choose to reduce the personality traits and habits that make you less charismatic. It's about accepting and making the most of your own unique, charismatic style.

The first step towards being authentic is to accept yourself for who you are. We often put a lot of pressure on ourselves to be perfect or part of the latest trend: the best employee, the perfect parent, the coolest friend.

The good news is that perfection isn't necessary to be charismatic. We're all constant works in progress, and the sooner you accept that the sooner you can relax and enjoy exploring your own unique, charismatic style. When you allow your true self to shine through, your charisma will develop quickly.

But what does being authentic mean? We've already discussed positive personality traits in Chapter 6. So, what if you don't think any of those traits are the 'authentic' you? Perhaps, for example, you believe you are naturally a negative or pessimistic person and that those traits are not compatible with being charismatic.

Luckily, negativity and pessimism aren't 'natural' states; they're learned ones. And so are most negative (and indeed, positive) personality traits. The trick is to identify what really makes you feel positive. Sometimes, we're quick to point out what we don't like. But if you flip it and concentrate on what you do like, then you'll quickly become more positive.

For example, if you don't like outdoorsy holidays and find hiking boring, then chances are that you love the buzz of a big city or the relaxed atmosphere of a spa. Ask yourself, what do you like instead of focusing on the things you don't? Make it a habit to concentrate on your likes. The next time a colleague tells you about their amazing hiking trip, you can appreciate that they are passionate about hiking in the same way you are passionate about other things, making it much easier to respond positively instead of looking bored.

Being charismatic requires you to be authentic, to elevate your unique personality and let it shine through. It also requires allowing yourself to be a little vulnerable.

But wait! Aren't charismatic people all confident and self-assured?
Wouldn't showing vulnerability be the exact opposite of that?

Not exactly. Vulnerability might not be something you

associate with charismatic people, but displaying appropriate vulnerability can really enhance people's perception of you for the better.

Nobody really wants to be seen as vulnerable. We usually see it as a weakness, something to avoid at all costs, especially in the workplace, where we usually believe that we need to avoid any weakness signs to get ahead. We tend to believe that most charismatic leaders are strong leaders—the ones who make no mistakes and accept no blame.

This view that you must avoid vulnerability at all costs seems to make perfect sense on the surface. However, when you dig a little deeper, it becomes clear that avoiding being vulnerable could be holding you back.

Some of our natural aversion to showing vulnerability is because we don't understand exactly what it really means to be vulnerable. Vulnerability means having the courage to handle challenges that life throws at you while accepting that they are challenges. It also means having the courage to admit when you might need help or make a mistake.

It doesn't mean you need to overshare, reveal too much personal information, or become attention-seeking. Sharing every fear and mistake you make at work isn't an example of being vulnerable and could damage your credibility.

However, vulnerability, applied the right way, can boost your charisma instead of harming it. How? By promoting a genuine human connection and warmth.

Vulnerability gives you the advantage of authenticity. Allowing your vulnerability to be visible makes people feel trusted. We instinctively recognize on some level when somebody's words are incongruous with how they actually feel.

Most of these intuitive insights happen on a subconscious level. We don't analyze them, but when we subconsciously recognize that a person's words and body language don't match, we start to question their trustworthiness.

So how can you show vulnerability without damaging your reputation and credibility?
Take responsibility for your mistakes – It's not our mistakes that define us; it's how we handle them. The key is to show you're doing whatever you can to put it right.
Ask for help if you need it – Asking for help can make you vulnerable by exposing your weakness. But it also demonstrates to your colleagues and managers that you put effective outcomes above your personal pride. That's a sign of a good and trustworthy employee.
Empathize with colleagues that you know are experiencing any emotional difficulties – Perhaps they've lost a loved one, or there's an illness in the family. Let them know that you understand how difficult their personal challenges must be.

When Interests Clash

In most cases, you'll find that there are common goals or interests, or at the very least, an overlap. However, occasionally you'll come up against situations in work where your goals and interests clash.

For example, if there's a limited departmental budget, and you want to use some for your team's project, but a colleague also wants to use the budget for a different project. Doing both would take the department over budget. In situations like this, there's no straightforward way to resolve the issue unless you can find a way to merge both projects or downsize both projects so that the budget can cover both.

Handling clashing interests will almost always require you to think outside the box – and often, that will mean that you need time to consider how to tackle the situation. Don't be afraid to ask for the time to think about it.

If you can't find a compromise or way around the clashing interests, then you'll need to identify whose need is greatest. You'll need to do this from the perspective of the business. On paper, which project is likely to bring bigger benefits to the business? If that's not yours, then you may need to step back and agree to pick up your project in another budget year or considerably reduce your scope.

If, after looking at it objectively, and you genuinely believe your need is greater, then you'll want to collect some evidence. Focus on how your project will provide a benefit for the business that is A) more urgent than theirs and/or B) more profitable or desirable. If getting the outcome you want means that you have to persuade the other party, then be extra careful that your evidence isn't making the other project look bad. Focus only on the positives of your own, and not the negatives of the other. Be willing to point out and accept the good points of the other project too.

Charismatic Work Behaviors

Charisma is about more than what you say; it's about what you do. Remember, people only view you as charismatic when they believe you are genuine. If your words and your actions aren't aligned, you won't be seen as a charismatic person, just glib and untrustworthy.

These are some specific behaviors that are common to charismatic people. Demonstrating these behaviors at work and outside it, too, will help to cement people's perception of you as charismatic.

Flexibility

Charismatic people are flexible not simply in terms of time but also in listening to others and adjusting their own plans and opinions accordingly.

Being flexible in terms of your ideas and reaching your goals can help you get along with others much better. It doesn't mean putting other people's goals before yours or always bending over backward to compromise. It simply means being willing to hear people out, change your mind if they have honestly convinced you, and be open to considering different ways of doing things.

You never hear a charismatic person say, 'but that's how we've always done it...' They're much more likely to say, 'great idea, let's give it a try,' or 'sounds really interesting – can you come back to me with some data on how that might work?' And one thing they rarely do is cut someone's ideas off with a blanket refusal. Even when they say no, they leave the other person feeling good.

Willingness to Listen

Charismatic people are good listeners who practice active listening to ease people and ensure that they understand what somebody is trying to tell them. They also demonstrate empathy for others, making people feel heard and understood.

A willingness to listen to other people – to their ideas, problems, and concerns- is a good trait to develop at work. You don't always have to agree with them, but it will give you valuable insight into how others feel and what motivates them. In turn, that will make it easier when you want to influence or persuade somebody effectively.

Of course, you're not just listening to them to gain an advantage. Every interaction with a colleague is an opportunity to make them feel good and to build trust—two key components of charisma.

Teamworking & Being Visible

Charismatic people at work are visible, and they work well in a team – mostly because they have good people skills. Some key tips for good teamwork:

Limit how often you use "I" when talking with your team – Using "We" fosters inclusiveness and a sense of teamwork.

Offer praise where it's due – If someone has done a great job - let them know. People love to be recognized for their hard work, so always give credit where it's due. If you want to use a colleague's words or ideas in a meeting when they aren't present, make sure you credit them. Stealing the ideas of others won't make you look good. But sharing them and giving credit makes you look like a team player and someone who can be trusted.

Always keep your promises – If there's a genuinely good reason you can't do something, open a conversation with the person expecting it as soon as possible.

Stay truthful – Charismatic people are trustworthy, so

making a point always to tell the truth. Of course, there's a limit – if the truth would be hurtful or damaging, then don't say anything at all. Or if it's confidential information that you can't share – then say so. But don't lie to your coworkers if you want them to trust you.

Following these tips will help you develop trust and rapport with your colleagues, which will enhance your charisma – and your career prospects.

Real Life Case Study – Hunter

Hunter was recently promoted to a management position and wanted to make a great first impression on his new team and colleagues. He'd always admired how another leader in the company used humor in meetings to relax everybody and easily hold their attention.
Hunter tried to implement this in his own staff meetings, but it just fell flat with his team. If anything, it had the opposite effect, and he couldn't understand why.

When speaking to his friends outside of work about the problem, they asked him to give examples of the humor he'd used. It was then that he realized he'd been using the same kind of humor that the other manager used - but that didn't really fit with his personality.
Because it wasn't his natural humor, his jokes felt awkward, and his body language was out of line with what he was saying. Instead of allowing his own natural humor to shine through, he'd been trying to adopt somebody else's. Which just wasn't authentic, and his team was picking up on that.

Hunter decided to try again but using appropriate humor that was more natural for him. This time, his team responded much better to his jokes, and he broke some of the ice. From this experience, Hunter learned that observing others is a great way to learn charisma. But to get anything of real value from that, you need to adapt the way others do something to a way that suits your own personality.

We've looked at communicating at work in this chapter, but we haven't really delved deep into some of the 'big' conversations you're likely to need to have at work – and also in your day-to-day life. In the next chapter, we'll look at handling powerful conversations with charisma.

Chapter 9 – Powerful Conversations with Anyone

"I think the power of persuasion would be the greatest superpower of all time."
Jenny Mollen

What Are Powerful Conversations?

Powerful conversations are the ones that make a difference. Persuading, influencing, or motivating someone around your way of thinking or to take any action that you need them to take.

We've all experienced these powerful conversations, and most of us have more than one example of having powerful conversations that didn't go well for us. Charisma can help you navigate these kinds of conversations with relative ease, bringing people round to your way of thinking and making powerful conversations much less painful.

Persuading

Persuasion is something of an essential life skill, but it's often misunderstood. Sometimes when people think of persuasion, they think of manipulation or sleazy sales tactics designed to force someone into a particular course of action.

Persuasion, however, is none of these things. It's simply about reaching a shared understanding and agreement. Once you achieve this, you can work together to reach a mutually beneficial outcome.

Here are some tips on being more persuasive:

Establish Credibility

If you're trying to persuade people about a topic that you have no qualifications or experience in, you will lack credibility from the beginning. Credibility is essential for getting other people to take your views seriously. If you were at a dinner party and discussing healthcare, would you find the opinion of a qualified medical doctor or the opinion of a car salesman more persuasive? The doctor would, of course, have much more credibility in this situation. If you were discussing cars, however, the salesman would have the upper hand.

You won't always have a specific qualification in the topic you're discussing, but having some credibility is essential if you want to persuade people. Being seen as knowledgeable in the topic makes you more persuasive.

Another way to boost credibility is by your relationships. If you have built a reputation as trustworthy and genuine, people will tend to see your arguments as more credible, even without concrete evidence of knowledge or expertise.

Common Ground

Another important element of persuasion is common ground. Finding common ground makes it easier to bring your audience to an agreement with you, rather than pushing them towards your position.

When you understand what common ground there is, you can ensure that you position your argument in a way that appeals to your audience. Basing your persuasion on what you know their interests and goals are. Essentially, it would be best if you made it clear what is in it for them. What will the benefit be to them (and make sure it's one they care about).

One common mistake people make when trying to persuade others is to assume that everyone will hold the same values and concerns. Again, this is where building relationships will help your persuasiveness and charisma. When you truly understand what matters to your audience, you can easily frame things to appeal to their real interests.

Provide Evidence

Persuasion isn't just a battle of wills and charisma. Even if you have a high level of charisma, you may not be able to persuade without providing evidence. Interestingly, the evidence you need isn't always factual or data-driven.

Graphs and numbers might provide evidence, but they don't often grab your audience where it matters – their emotions. Factual data and information are certainly important but illustrating that data with vivid metaphors and anecdotes or relating it to real, everyday life, and what matters to your audience is how you truly persuade.

Create an Emotional Connection

This is where authenticity and vulnerability can really pack a punch when it comes to persuading. Appealing to your audience's emotions gives you a huge advantage. If you're passionate about something, then let that show.

Emotions can be positive or negative. You can persuade by creating a fear of something – perhaps a fear of missing out on a great opportunity. Or you can tap into more positive emotions like a sense of belonging and appeal to people's need for status.

Of course, it has to be matched with the audience's needs and interests. You want to bring them along with you, not alienate them. But when you do it right, you will nail persuading people. Emotions are a big factor in how we make decisions. Without connecting with people's emotions, even the strongest arguments can fail to persuade.

Influencing

Influencing is like persuading but is often more subtle. When you're persuading someone, it's usually obvious that you want to bring them around to your way of thinking. Influencing is slightly more subtle.

There are two styles of influencing – pull and push. Both of these are valid styles, but you'll need to read the situation and the person properly before choosing a style. Most of us naturally lean towards either a push or pull style, but adapting to either has huge advantages.

Pull styles use a straightforward, assertive approach, for example, by using data, facts, and figures to literally 'pull' another towards the outcome you want. You can also similarly use emotions to push people towards an outcome. This is very different from emotional manipulation and usually involves you leading from the front with passion, which pulls others behind you.

Push styles are more passive. You might still use facts and figures, but simply by laying them out and then letting people decide. You could also use an emotional approach, but a more collaborative one, listening to people and encouraging them – pushing them from behind into action rather than pulling them along behind you.

The best style to use will depend on the situation.

Charismatic people tend to know how to use either style to suit the situation but will often use a collaborative approach when they can.

Motivating

Charismatic people are great motivators. They can keep people excited and inspired, motivated to achieve something.

The first key is being self-motivated themselves. If you aren't passionate and motivated, then it's tough to inspire others. The second key is understanding people and what makes them tick. There are two basic types of motivation – internal and external. Internal motivation is very personal, whereas external motivation is based on factors like salary, bonuses, holidays, and other tangible rewards.

A lot of companies and managers rely on external motivators to keep employees motivated. However, internal motivation can actually be much more powerful. The best kind of motivation encompasses both to keep it balanced.

Encouraging internal motivation means that you need to understand what drives people, and it will be different things for different people. There's no one size fits all approach to motivation. To effectively motivate, it needs a tailored approach as much as possible. In many cases, one powerful way to motivate people is simply listening to their frustrations and concerns and doing what you can to remove obstacles and make their jobs easier.

Of course, it's not limited to work. You can use similar techniques in your personal life. For example, you can motivate your spouse to become healthier by tapping into their internal motivators – being healthy for their family or looking good at a party. You can also offer external motivators such as rewards for reaching certain milestones.

Directing & Controlling Conversations

Charismatic people are good at directing and controlling conversations. That doesn't mean that they are the ones doing all of the talking, but they are the ones that keep the conversation on track, driving it towards the right outcome.

In most cases, this means asking the right questions. Asking the right question is crucial for effective communications. Using the right questions in any situation, you can gain better information, build stronger relationships, and manage people more effectively.

It's also important to keep the conversation on the topic. Most of the time, if you're asking the right questions, the conversation will stay on topic. It's natural to veer off topic slightly and then come back, but if the conversations seem to be going in a different direction than you want, you'll need to be skilled at bringing it back on track.

Questions are one of the most effective tools for keeping a conversation on track. The trick is to ask the right kind of questions to ensure the conversation flows the way you want it. But how many types of questions are there?

Open Questions

Open questions are great for starting a conversation or for

gathering information. An open question usually begins with 'What' 'Why' or 'How,' and they always elicit more than a 'yes' or 'no' answer. They tend to be difficult to answer in just one word, encouraging others to provide information.

Examples of open questions are:
- What happened yesterday?
- How did you research the project?
- Why did you decide on this particular color?
- What do you think about this idea?

Open questions are great for starting a more open-ended conversation or gathering facts.

Closed Questions
Closed questions tend to elicit a 'yes' or 'no' response, or sometimes simply a terse response.

Examples of closed questions are:
- Did you bring a pen?
- What time is the meeting tomorrow?
- Are you hungry?

Closed questions are not usually beneficial to encouraging conversation, but they are useful for clarifying or checking your understanding of something.

Leading Questions
Leading questions are designed to elicit a specific response. They're worded so that you are leading the person towards a certain assumption or answer.

For example:
- How many of these do you want?
- Option two fits your needs best, doesn't it?

   -   How do you want me to bill you for that?

Leading questions have a place, but overuse can make you seem pushy and manipulative, so use them wisely.

Funnel Questions

Funnel questions are more of a technique than a type of question. They can be open or closed but tend to start with open questions and finish with more closed questions that elicit shorter answers. These are the type of questions and questioning techniques we might associate with lawyers or police officers, and they're excellent for getting specific detail.

The following is an example of funnel questions and potential answers.

"Who was at the meeting yesterday?"
"Andrew, Sarah, David, Melanie, and Mark."
"What was discussed?"
"We went through the outstanding projects and any blockers."
"Did anybody mention the Smithfield project?"
"No."
"Which projects were discussed?"
"Horton and Makin. Sarah said that the Horton project should be finished next week."
"Any mention of when the Makin project will be finished?"
"Mark estimated another two months,"
"Do you agree with that estimate?"
"Yes."

Funnel questions are good when trying to get to the specific detail of something, but they can feel a bit too rapid-fire if they continue for too long.

Probing Questions

Probing questions, look for more information or clarification on something. They're handy when someone seems to be avoiding telling you something. Asking them probing questions makes it difficult for them not to mention something that you need to know. They tend to be a little more open-ended than funnel questions, although they are closely related.

- Tell me more about what happened at the meeting?
- How did you know that the Smithfield project was running over budget?
- How would you approach that differently next time?
- Talk me through your thought process on the Makin account?

Rhetorical Questions

Rhetorical questions don't actually need or expect an answer, but you can use them to engage your audience and drive them towards a particular conclusion.

A Rhetorical question is actually a statement but phrased as though it is a question:
- Sarah's really efficient, isn't she?
- This is a lovely color, isn't it?
- How long are we going to wait before we take action?

Using the most appropriate questioning technique can help you control the conversation. You can learn more about a person or situation by asking open and probing questions. You can clarify something with closed or funnel questions, and you can make a point using rhetorical questions.

Using questions effectively requires good active listening skills. People will tire quickly of questions if they feel their answers aren't being listened to. Paying attention to your own and others' body language and tone can also help put your audience at ease to answer the questions honestly.

Closing Powerful Conversations

The following tips are all sales techniques designed to get prospects to make a purchase. Although they are sales techniques, they can also be relevant to any other situations where you want someone to decide. When you've put all the hard work into influencing and persuading, you don't want your audience to walk away without having fully invested in the outcome. If they do, your attempts to persuade or influence may fail.

Create A Sense Of Urgency
If people believe they have a long time to make a decision, they will potentially want to use that time to think about it. If you need a decision fast, one way to close a conversation is to create a sense of urgency.

This is about making it urgent for them, not telling them that it is urgent for you. For example, there might be an offer discount, but they will need to decide sooner rather than later if the discount ends today.

This is a pretty effective technique, but it will only work if the other person believes that the offering is valuable. If you haven't fully established buy-in with persuading and influencing skills, it won't work.

Summarize The Conversation

This is a good way to close the conversation if the other person has already indicated that they are interested in what is offered. Essentially, you are simply summarizing the conversation's key points – focusing mainly on the benefits or what's in it for the other person and then finishing with an assumptive question.

For example:
"So, we're going to install the premium package that includes a month's free insurance. What date would you like the payments to start?"

Questions

Questions aren't just good for directing a conversation. They're also great tools to close them as well. For example, "Does what we just discussed appeal to you?" or "Is there anything on your side preventing us from moving forward with this quickly?"

By asking for their opinion or clarifying any challenges, you can move on quickly to signing on the dotted line or solving any problems.

Cautious Closing

This is a softer approach that doesn't make any assumptive demands. It's another closing technique that uses questions to move the conversation towards a close. This time, it's a low-impact, closed question.

The trick here is also to include what's in it for the other person. For example:

"If I said I could reduce your overheads by 10% over the next 6 months, would you want to hear more?"

This leaves it open for the other person to say no and doesn't pressure them into anything.

We've covered how to have powerful conversations and influence, persuade and motivate people. One common theme across all of these is that you absolutely need to understand people and build a relationship before finding it easy to do these things.

Chapter 10 – Managing Conflict Charismatically

"For good ideas and true innovation, you need human interaction, conflict, argument, debate."
Margaret Heffernan

Types of Conflict

Conflict is something we tend to think of as negative, even something to avoid. But conflict is natural. Without conflict, there would be no big changes or challenges to the status quo, and nothing would ever change.

Charismatic people don't avoid conflict, but they don't actively seek it out either. They do, however, recognize it for what it is – an opportunity. Conflict generally arises when the goals of two or more parties don't match.

Of course, not all kinds of conflict are positive. A drunk in a bar starting a fight doesn't usually represent an opportunity for positive change – and there are some conflicts that it makes sense to avoid. But many conflicts – especially the ones we encounter at work – are actually a good thing.

In the workplace, there are three common types of conflict: task conflict, relationship conflict, and value conflict.

Task Conflict

Task conflict is when a disagreement arises between employees and colleagues based on who should complete that work. Task conflict usually happens when their tasks or priorities aren't aligned, or one party considers their work to be of a higher status. For example, if there's a high-profile client, you may have several people wanting to work on their project over and above other projects. There could be a conflict about who should work on which projects.

Task conflict can also arise between departments, where one department feels they are not consulted on decisions that affect their department. For example, if a production line manager decided to adjust the quality assurance process without consulting the quality management team, it would likely cause a conflict.

Task conflict is a great opportunity to tackle 'silo' working in a business. Silos are where teams or individuals don't share information, goals, tools, priorities, or processes with other teams within the same business. Silo working can lead to work duplication and prevents efficient and effective working across the business. It's the opposite of a collaborative working style.

Silo working prevents good decision making and good teamwork, and it's rarely an effective way to work. It usually comes about due to a business culture where employees aren't encouraged to share knowledge. It can be prevalent in businesses with a history of laying off staff. In these cases, people become protective of their knowledge, believing that they need to keep it to themselves to remain 'necessary' to the business.

Unfortunately, the silo mentality rarely makes anybody more employable or less at risk from job cuts. It can even hinder people in developing the teamwork skills essential to finding work after being laid off. Collaborative workers, on the other hand, don't need to be as afraid of job cuts because their collaborative working style makes them both valuable to their current employer and valuable to any new employer.

If task conflicts arise frequently, it can be a sign that there's a silo mentality that needs tackling to improve productivity and increase staff engagement.

Task type of conflict is less likely to arise if policies and procedures are open and transparent, employees are encouraged to share knowledge, and if employees and departments feel that they are consulted on decisions that affect them.

Relationship Conflict
Relationship conflict is when people have different personalities that may not mesh well together. This kind of conflict can happen anywhere, but it's common in the workplace where people who wouldn't ordinarily seek each other out are expected to work closely together.

Relationship conflicts are often seen at a management level, where employees feel that their manager does not behave comfortably. For example, someone who finds coarse language offensive would potentially be very uncomfortable with a manager who used curse words casually in the workplace.

Relationship conflicts can be a great opportunity to build and strengthen working relationships. Often, if both parties can find their common ground, they can build from there to good mutual respect and tolerance. These kinds of conflicts can often be avoided if there is enough emphasis placed on team building and if each employee or colleague is expected to treat others equally.

Not all relationship conflicts can, or should be, solved. In the case of active bullying where there is strong evidence that the conflict arises because of clearly inappropriate behavior from one party, then following normal company HR procedures for those situations would be advised.

Value Conflict

Value conflict is where people's culture, religion, politics, and ethics can cause disagreements. People can feel very strongly about their personal values, and when those of a colleague clash with yours, it can lead to conflict.

These can be some of the most difficult conflicts to handle, as both parties often feel very passionate about their own personal values. And often, there's no obvious 'right' or 'wrong' solution. An example of this might be seen when discussing who will work over holiday periods. Some colleagues with young families will feel very strongly that family commitments should entitle them to particular days off, over and above their single colleagues. In comparison, their single colleagues without those ties might object to what they see as a sense of entitlement and feel that they should be given equal priority for time off.

Both sides will tend to be very passionate about their stance on the matter, but a charismatic leader should bring both sides to a compromise. In fact, charismatic people would embrace this kind of conflict as a chance to listen to both sides and create a fair and transparent policy for all employees, preventing this kind of conflict from reoccurring.

Handling Conflict

Sometimes we know we are likely to encounter conflict, and sometimes it comes out of the blue and surprises us. Luckily, there are ways to handle any conflict to ensure that it doesn't get out of hand, and both parties can leave a conversation feeling satisfied that they have been listened to.

If you know you are likely to encounter conflict, preparing beforehand is a good idea. What kind of concerns and objections do you expect the other person to raise? Having this prepared and considering their potential concerns will help you keep the conversation on track and even pre-emptively address some of those concerns.

How will you show that you have considered and listened to them? Remember that a charismatic person makes others feel good. It might not always be possible in a conflict situation, but you are more likely to gain someone's trust and respect by actively listening to them – even if you still don't agree or concede.

If you can't prepare, or if something takes you by surprise during the conversation, don't be afraid to park some issues. Not everything has to be resolved immediately. If a concern or topic is brought up that you can't tackle at that moment, simply by acknowledging it and agreeing on a time to revisit it, you can move past that particular concern and focus on the ones you can tackle time.

You must return to it within the timeframe you agreed if you park an issue. Using 'parking' as a way to push issues or concerns out of the discussion will result in people losing trust in you. If you attempted it again, they may even strongly resist putting it to one side at all. Parking is a much more powerful tool when you have gained trust.

How To Understand and Tackle Conflict

Conflict is usually driven by one of our five core concerns. These represent our basic human desires in most interactions. By focusing on these core concerns, you can reduce the length of any conflict and ensure that any conversation goes as smoothly as possible.

The five core concerns are appreciation, affiliation, autonomy, status, and role.

Appreciation

We all like to feel appreciated, and demonstrating appreciation can resolve a conflict and stop it from occurring in the first place. Demonstrating appreciation involves understanding and valuing the other person's point of view.

The best way to demonstrate appreciation is to show that you can see the value of the other person's words, actions, or emotions. For example, in the earlier conflict example about time off over the holiday period, you could acknowledge both sides frustrations:

To employee 1: *"I understand that the holidays are a special time when you have a young family, and it's important for you to have some quality family time with them."*

To employee 2: *"I also understand that the holidays are a time for you to relax and to visit with your family. And not having children doesn't mean that the holidays aren't a special time for you too."*

To both employees: *"I'm sure there's a way we can work around the situation and ensure that nobody has to miss out on their own holiday traditions. How do you see the way forward with this?"*

Demonstrating that you understand and value their feelings about the situation before you try and solve the problem reduces the tension. It also demonstrates that both employees are being taken seriously. This will make them much more open to a compromise.

Affiliation
Applying affiliation involves encouraging a collaborative approach. This detracts from the 'me' vs. 'you' conflict dynamic and tries to turn the situation into a team effort to solve a problem - making it an 'us' dynamic.

To apply affiliation, you'll need to find some common ground. Look for what you do have in common, or try to use small talk to reinforce common interests. The more related to the conflict, the better, but any common ground is good. Shared sporting interests, television shows, mutual friends. Anything that demonstrates the ways you are similar will help to build an affiliation.

This is where getting into the habit of switching 'I' and 'you' for 'we' and 'us' really helps. This way, you can build and maintain a picture of both parties working collaboratively and not separately.

Autonomy
We all also have a desire to feel that we are in control of our own lives. Many conflicts occur because people feel they have been overlooked in decisions or actions that have impacted them, just like our earlier example of the quality team not being consulted about a change in the quality process.

You can address autonomy by consulting others before

taking any actions that might impact them, but it isn't easy to resolve if this step hasn't already been taken. Unfortunately, you may not realize that your actions or decisions impact someone until it's too late. Thinking through carefully who might be affected when making any large decisions is always a good habit to build.

If there's a conflict relating to autonomy, then a good way to resolve it is to apologize and ask how they think you can resolve the conflict.

Status

Status is about our need to be recognized for our strengths and achievements. When people feel that their sense of status is being challenged, they can become defensive or aggressive. People who feel that they have an elevated status can become arrogant or attempt to 'bulldoze' other people – leading to conflict.

Leveraging your perceived status in a conflict isn't a particularly charismatic thing to do. It can lead to the other person becoming very resentful and can damage relationships. You can positively use status during conversations by deferring to the other person's expertise or asking their advice.

To resolve conflict charismatically, try and avoid allowing a disagreement to become a battle over status. Find common ground, acknowledge the other person's opinion and expertise, and try and work collaboratively.

Apologizing Charismatically

When conflict is involved, there will inevitably be some times where you are on the wrong side of the conflict and need to apologize. Being wrong doesn't have to affect your charisma. In fact, in many cases, it can be a positive boost to how people perceive you – as long as you handle the apology properly.

No matter how embarrassing your mistake may seem, you can still come out of the situation with your dignity – and charisma - intact. It's a rare trait for people to own their mistakes and apologize for them properly. Most people are so bad at apologies that just by doing it right, you can stand out for all the right reasons, and the chances are that the other person will forget the original mistake quickly. In contrast, the positive impact of a good apology will live on.

The first step to apologizing properly is to take a moment to forgive yourself. It's easy to beat yourself up when you get something wrong, but it's not necessary. Accept your mistake, own it, and forgive yourself.

Forgiving yourself is important for several reasons:

A positive mindset is essential to being charismatic, and having a positive mindset is difficult when you're holding your mistakes over your head.
Beating yourself up about a mistake can make you over-apologize and come across as too apologetic, or even worse, it can make you come across as defensive about the mistake.

You can't change it. Whatever the mistake is, you can't rewind time. All you can do is move forward positively, right whatever you can, and own the mistake. Being hard on yourself won't undo the mistake, and it won't help you put right what you can – so let it go.

Once you're in the right mindset and have forgiven yourself, the second step is to make an apology. Consider the best way to communicate your apology. For most situations, in-person is best wherever possible. As we learned in Chapter 7, a large portion of our communication is non-verbal. An in-person apology allows you to demonstrate via body language and facial expressions the sincerity of your apology, giving it extra gravitas.

In some cases, you won't be able to make an in-person apology. In these instances, a video call is often the next-best option. A video call will allow you still to convey some elements of body language and facial expressions. It also gives you the advantage of seeing and interpreting the other person's non-verbal response and adapting your own response if needed.

A telephone call is another option, but you will need to rely on your words and tone of voice to convey sincerity. You also won't get any non-visual clues about how well your apology is being received.

In writing is your final option. For this option, you won't have the ability to use or read any non-verbal clues at all. You will need to consider wording and tone extremely carefully as the person receiving it will have only the words in front of them to identify tone and intent. In some cases, the mood of the person receiving the message can heavily impact how they perceive the tone and intent.

Written does have some advantages, however. You will have time to consider and rewrite your words before sending them, and it's a formal method of communication that can lend some weight to your apology.

Your decision on which method to choose will need to consider your own preferences and, more importantly, your best guess on the other person's preferences. If in doubt, aim for face-to-face where possible.

The Actual Apology

Approach the apology by understanding how any mistake may have impacted the other person and how you can put it right.

Depending on the mistake, the apology doesn't have to be long or verbose. Often simpler is better. In many cases, a simple and sincere 'I'm sorry' and an acknowledgment of your mistake's impact on the other person is enough.

If you made a big mistake, and there's a good explanation as to why you made a mistake and a good reason it won't happen again, then say that. However, there's a big difference between an explanation and an excuse. An explanation is an honest account of how and why the mistake happened. An excuse attempts to shift the blame or escape accountability.

Be open to honest feedback from the other person and be willing to hear them out about how the mistake has impacted them and any suggestions on how you can put things right.

Remember the three key components of charisma from Chapter 1? Presence, power, and warmth. Employing these three principles in your apology will help you make a charismatic apology. When listening to the other person, display warmth in acknowledging your mistake and the impact on the other person, and display power in your conviction to put the mistake right.

Conflict is an unavoidable fact of life, but when you learn how to handle conflict properly, it can really boost how charismatic you seem to others.

Conclusion

We've covered all the critical aspects of becoming more charismatic, from identifying what charisma is – and isn't, to assessing your current charisma levels and exploring actionable tips to increase that count.

Here's a quick recap of the key points we've covered:

- Charisma is a collection of sophisticated social and emotional skills. When you increase these skills, it can stir strong emotions in other people while also projecting exceptional calm, confidence, and focus.

- Being mindful and aware of your body language can help you become instantly more charismatic. It also means you can read and react to other people's emotions more effectively. Understanding body language gives you a significant insight into what others may be thinking or feeling.

- The most charismatic kind of communication is assertive, and I've covered some tips and techniques to help you become a more assertive communicator, such as active listening.

  By becoming a more active listener, you not only hear what's being said, but you will also now notice the way the messages are communicated. You know to read between the lines of a conversation, to pick up all the verbal and non-verbal cues for extra information because this is essential to understanding the whole message the speaker is trying to get across.

- You should be developing certain personality traits like patience, tolerance, respect, and trust to also increase your charisma levels. Making those behaviors a habit will make it much easier to be effortlessly charismatic. You also know that it makes sense to concentrate on building good behavioral habits –one at a time– to provide a cornerstone for your charismatic personality.

- Having the right mindset is vital for charisma. People are attracted to and captivated by positivity and success. When you have the right mindset, you will become naturally attractive to others and more likely to hold their attention.

- Charisma helps you handle powerful conversations with ease. It allows you to persuade, influence, and even close sales with ease, without resorting to underhanded tactics.

- Conflict is a necessary part of communicating with others, but it doesn't have to be stressful. By understanding the different types of conflict, and the five core concerns, you know that you can quickly resolve most disputes without damaging your charisma.

- Accepting mistakes and effectively apologizing can boost your charisma – so there's no need to be afraid of making a mistake now and then.

Developing charisma is an incredible way of boosting your success, both in the workplace and in your personal relationships. Remember, charisma is simply a set of skills you can learn if you are willing to put in the time and effort.

Now that you know how to become more charismatic, it's time to put that learning into practice and become the very best version of yourself.

www.ingramcontent.com/pod-product-compliance
Lightning Source LLC
Chambersburg PA
CBHW070552220526
45467CB00003B/1178